When women are trying to cope with a problem, struggling through a major life transition, or just in need of a reality check and a little healing support, we go straight to our friends. Each of the books in the *Women Talk About* series reflects the experiences of dozens of women from diverse backgrounds, whose words are accompanied by provocative insights from the latest research. Often funny, sometimes painful, and always honest, their powerful voices reassure us that we're not alone, offer guidance and wisdom, and show us how to connect back to the woman we want to be.

the
Deepest Blue

how women face &
overcome depression

LAUREN DOCKETT

Foreword by Matthew McKay, Ph.D.

New Harbinger Publications, Inc.

Publisher's Note

This publication is designed to provide accurate and authoritative information in regard to the subject matter covered. It is sold with the understanding that the publisher is not engaged in rendering psychological, financial, legal, or other professional services. If expert assistance or counseling is needed, the services of a competent professional should be sought.

Distributed in the U.S.A. by Publishers Group West; in Canada by Raincoast Books; in Great Britain by Airlift Book Company, Ltd.; in South Africa by Real Books, Ltd.; in Australia by Boobook; and in New Zealand by Tandem Press.

Copyright © 2001 by Lauren Dockett
New Harbinger Publications, Inc.
5674 Shattuck Avenue
Oakland, CA 94609

Cover design by Amy Shoup
Edited by Heather Garnos
Text design by Spencer Smith

Library of Congress number: 01-132282
ISBN 1-57224-253-1 Paperback

Printed in the United States of America

New Harbinger Publications' Web site address:
www.newharbinger.com

03   02   01

10   9   8   7   6   5   4   3   2   1

First printing

to Vishnupriya and Alyson
for all the hope they evoke

Contents

Acknowledgments

Thanks to all the women who shared their deeply personal stories with me. This is their book. Love to the brave members of my family whose own love and example continue to sustain me through all shadings of my mood: my sister Susan, mother Pat and father Doc, and my incomparable cousins Tecia Breen-Bond and Donald and Cindy Breen. To the friends who stayed steadfast with me: Taleen Kadamian, Jan York, Loura Howey, Deena Solwren, Leon Porter, Maria Dea, Evelyn Cohen, Kate Megregian, and my extended Bay Area family, I can never say thank you enough. Hugs to Kristin Beck and Andy Liotta, my beloved titlers, and to Amy Shoup and Julie Feinstein, for making art out of it all. Very special thanks to Catharine Sutker and Matthew McKay for their support and enhancement of the work, and to Heather Garnos, for her enthusiasm and seamless editing. My thanks to the New Harbingerites who make it sound and look so good, including Michele Waters, Spencer Smith, Kirk Johnson, Gretchen Gold, and Kasey Pfaff. And finally, my love and thanks to Stephen Gilbert, Jr., for the readings and whatnot.

Foreword

It's an honor for me to introduce *The Deepest Blue* to you.
This unique and important book can be a companion, even
a guide, to help you navigate the dark waters of depression. By its nature, depression is isolating. The world
seems to go on without you while you slip further and further from the human anchors of your life. The old con-
nections, the friends and family who were once sources of
nourishment, seem harder to reach now. Harder to stay
close to. Many of them can't begin to understand what
you're facing, so you start to hunger for the people who
have been there. You want companions who know what
depression is like, but who have somehow gotten to the
other side.

The Deepest Blue is a chance to meet women who
have made this journey before you. Their voices have the
resonance of authenticity because they know depression
from the inside. Theirs isn't clinical or shrink knowledge—though shrinks would be wise to listen to it—but
awareness grown from the daily struggle to understand and
overcome their own depression.

The women who speak from the pages of this beautifully written book can tell you things no therapist, no
uninitiated friend, could ever say. They talk about what
it's like as the feelings of sadness, detachment, and help-

lessness first overwhelm them. How it feels to be diagnosed. Some describe the sense of stigma. Others, a relief at finally having found an explanation for the pain.

The women in *The Deepest Blue* tell everything they did to make the crossing. How they coped. How they found meaning and spiritual rebirth. How they learned to manage, even change the nature of the pain. There are secrets in the book, purchased at great price, and offered with an open, casual grace. Women talk directly, as if in the company of friends, about what caused their depression, about how depression changes relationships, about how depression can be a signal that some relationships *need* to change. Women talk about their experience with medications, with doctors and hospitals, with charlatans and true healers.

But the core of this book is how so many women have found ways to heal themselves. From old abuse and pain, from the confinement of unfulfilling roles, from emptiness and disconnection, from loss. They have found ways to strengthen a sense of self, change old negative beliefs and attitudes, and honor their true life path.

What you'll read here confirms what you already know. There is nothing easy about this crossing. But each of these women has been out there where you are. You are not alone. Together, the voices in this book will give you courage—and a map. The crossing is hard, but Lauren Dockett and the women of *The Deepest Blue* will show you how to reach the other side.

Matthew McKay, Ph.D.
Author of *Self-Esteem* and *Thoughts & Feelings*

Illness is the night-side of life, a more onerous citizenship. Everyone who is born holds dual citizenship, in the kingdom of the well and in the kingdom of the sick. Although we all prefer to use only the good passport, sooner or later each of us is obliged, at least for a spell, to identify ourselves as citizens of that other place.

—Susan Sontag

Introduction

Depression is a deserter. It feels, as one of the women I interviewed says, "as if your brain has betrayed you." Those of us who have experienced depression know how painful the absence of ourselves during a depressive episode can be. When you're depressed, your mind ends up a lonely defector, wandering around unconnected to all that you'd previously known and felt. The kicker is that in the midst of all of this wandering, you rarely come upon anything useful. Instead, you find yourself suffering in a kind of wintry solitude that is home to the yammering undercurrent of your disconnected self.

As someone who's considered suicide, taken antidepressants, met with therapists and social workers and psychiatrists of every conceivable denomination, tried herbs and prayer and acupuncturists, sat in hospital-sponsored depression groups, and tossed and turned on the couches and in the guest rooms of countless concerned family members and friends, I can now cut a wide and knowledgeable swath through the common symptoms of this defecting state.

In the depths of my depressive world I've been awake for weeks at a time, and alternately found sleep such a blanketing drug that nothing—not food, not a bellyful of pee, not the glaring California sun scalding my face—could rouse me. I have become one with couch throws and the television and hokey movies and junk food. And at other times I have developed hypochondriacal aversions to almost everything I put past my lips; as well as to wonderful friends and potential lovers, and a long list of public places—not the least of which was the sidewalk beyond my front gate. I, like many depressed women, have had close friends tell me that I am too much for them in this state, that they can do nothing for me, that before they'd seen me like this I had always seemed so strong and normal. And I have watched them turn with little more than a quick shiver of guilt and walk forever away.

This is a book that reaches beyond the limitations of my personal experience. There are countless depression experts out there. And according to today's researchers, a full two-thirds of them are women. I've found thirty of these women and in these pages many of them tell the stories of how their depressions came to be, what they mean for them and how they change them, and how they in their individual worlds have learned to cope with and finally overcome even the deepest blues. It can be enormously helpful for depressed people to hear the truth of each other's experience. As one interviewee says, "Depression is living in a different world from most people," and that world can make many sufferers feel utterly lost and alone. Here though are thirty women who know the difference between empathy and sympathy. Who I've seen abandon platitudes in the presence of one another and watch, fearless and knowing, as dreams of death and tales of dissolution are confessed. Some were in the midst of depressions when we talked, some were between episodes, and still others said that their depressions were far enough behind them to be considered finally over, but still haunting enough that they were easily remembered and described in detail. A number of the women I spoke with have been hospitalized for their depressions. Quite a few have contemplated or attempted suicide, and many have used large quantities of illicit drugs and alcohol to dull their pain. Some have not done any of these things, but may instead have been laid low by their depressions in more subtle ways. Some have suffered from depression for as long as they can remember; others had a bout or two or three that they are still able to recall with brilliant clarity. The women, were they all to be given clinical diagnoses, would find that they exhibit symptoms ranging from the mildest "adjustment disorder" to full-scale major depression. Their actual diagnoses, however, seemed to have little bearing on the conversations that took place. More important were the enlightening descriptions of depressions and the tools we need to recover from them. These were remarkably similar.

The experience of talking to so many people about the intimacies of thought and mood has been wonderfully moving. These women wanted very much to share whatever they could about their experience. At the same time that I've encountered great openness on their part, I've run into a good deal of wariness when describing this book to friends and strangers. Peoples' discomfort gets most palpable when I out myself as having experienced depression. I'm unsure at these times if what I'm feeling from them is merely a sense of surprise that I've gone ahead and admitted it, or if I am forcing an intimacy that they'd rather not enter into—forcing an issue that they'd rather not face. I realize that sometimes people who haven't had a significant depression honestly don't understand it. In his masterful memoir *Darkness Visible*, William Styron describes this as a kind of healthy person's indifference. When recalling a visit to a depressed friend that was made when he himself was still well, Styron says, "This memory of my relative indifference is important because such indifference demonstrates powerfully the outsider's inability to grasp the essence of the illness. . . . (my friends' depressions) were abstract ailments to me, in spite of my sympathy, and I hadn't an inkling of (the) true contours or the nature of the pain so many victims experience as the mind continues its insidious meltdown" (25–26). A part of this reality Styron attributes to the indescribability of the depressive state: ". . . it has to be emphasized that if the pain were readily describable most of the countless sufferers from this ancient affliction would have been able to confidently depict for their friends and loved ones (even their physicians) some of the actual dimensions of their torment, and perhaps elicit a comprehension that has been generally lacking; such incomprehension has usually been due not to a failure of sympathy but to the basic inability of healthy people to imagine a form of torment so alien to everyday experience" (16–17).

Part of the beauty of writing this kind of book is coming into contact with people who can comprehend this "indescribable" state. It is still difficult for me not to marvel at a person of a certain age who can say that he or she has never been depressed. I find myself watching such people carefully and wondering what they know. Do they truly hold the secrets to perpetual, undisturbed wellness? Or are they coasting on chance? Sometimes I think they are blessed. At other times I think untouched, maybe a little hollow. Whatever their reality may be, as someone who has been knocked flat by depression, I've grown to prefer the company and wisdom of those who've fallen as far as I have. It's they that I truly believe in. More than the drugs, the groups, the therapists, and the morning runs, it is they who have gotten me well.

A few years ago, soon after the completion of my first book, I treated myself to a trip overseas. I chose a developing country, hoping that I'd find a renewed sense of strength and purpose in my role as intrepid traveler. Instead I got a potentially fatal tropical disease and found a renewed sense of pain and suffering. When I got home I went crazy enough to reach out for help. Help from doctors. Help from therapists. Help, with little hesitation on my part, from drugs. I wanted the professionals this time. Those people who with their magical hold on chemistry and cognition knew all the ways of keeping people like me alive. What I found in the wake of their work was a quiet kind of recognition that I could not make it through all of life's fall-downs unassisted. Letting go of that superficial sense of strength has done me a great deal of good. It has brought me into an unthinkable closeness with those I love. It has treated me to incredible bouts of honesty from people who have recognized my dangerous state of mind and hurriedly confessed their own. It has helped me understand and look with love upon those people in my life who have chosen not to live. And it has taught me that "losing it" is one of the few things in life that will bring you the capacity for true compassion. The women whom I've talked to and those who have made it into this book share these capacities, and have, moreover, stronger and more helpful insights than most professionals I've met.

This is not to say that depression is good. And I won't venture to say that anyone is oh-so-grateful for the experience of it. I for one hate who I am when I'm depressed. The misconception of depressives as overly indulgent both irks and makes sense to me. I am easily sick of myself after a day of wallowing behavior. In those early days of an episode, it often feels that I am selfishly choosing to fall apart. After all, I'll shout to my slipping self, it wasn't always this way! At one point there was joy and certainty and so much fun and laughter that I felt nothing but distant pity for my friends and family who I knew to be depressed. I'd decided I was never going be that way. I, doo-da-doo, was an optimist.

The women you'll meet struggle with shifting philosophical ideas about their depressive state. One of the appealing things about depression for many of us is the feeling we get that we're closer to some essential truth when we're down. That easing into pessimism and pain is a journey of some higher order. That we're learning through our suffering. It's a concept that works. Pain as teacher. Easterners have been all over this idea for generations. And understanding the whys of suffering can seem all the more plausible to us when we're mired in it.

But while we try to make sense of it, and mine it for the riches we're certain it must contain, let's not forget to acknowledge the ironically humdrum nature of the depressive experience. The millions of people, since time immemorial, who have lived it; the cultures that consider it such a regular happening that they never even bother to come up with a word to describe it. And the rather preposterous way that we in the States have made it into something just short of shocking, and assigned to it the status of disease.

Still it's important to balance this interest in the possible "neutrality" or even "necessity" of depression in the life experience with the reality that it is so much more a part of a woman's experience than it is a man's. I'm still taken aback by the gender disparity in the statistics of depression diagnosis. Study after study confirms it: a full two women to every one man. Is there something inherent in our society that contributes to women's higher numbers? Does this unfortunate reality have to do with oppression or enforced limitations or ill treatment? Is there some cruel genetic or hormonal or developmental issue that predisposes women and girls to torturous moods? Some of the older women I spoke with, who have suffered repeatedly with depression and have watched mothers and sisters and daughters and friends suffer as well, have come to view depression as another inevitable condition or consequence of their sex.

There are researchers who believe that depression is in fact shared more equally between the sexes but that for various reasons women are more often diagnosed and receiving treatment. More recent research finds that men and women exhibit different coping mechanisms, and that even if the diagnostic numbers are not valid, the treatment should still be specific to gender. After reviewing what is still very inconclusive literature on the sex differences in depression, I asked these thirty women to answer for themselves and their sex: Why us? I also took a look at the current drug, therapy, and health/nutrition/exercise/stress reduction literature and asked the group to tell me whether what they see available to them in terms of treatment is sufficiently responsive to the needs of women. Some spoke about alternatives to conventional treatment and about the role of spirituality in their own healing, while others were diehard drug fans.

We also discussed what it's like when you start to reach out to others, be they family or friends or professionals, when you're down. About how integral isolation and self-hatred are to prolonging depression, and what it feels like when you discover that not only are you not on your own, but the number of others suffering in just your "indescribable" way is huge.

The treatment of depression is in an interesting place these days. With the current prevailing view that depression is a purely biological disorder, we are sometimes averse to look at the circumstances in our life that may contribute to how we feel and to the possible deeper meaning inherent in the experience of depression.

In the course of these discussions, vivid descriptions of the depressive state emerged, and some of the mystery of where it all comes from and why it hangs around was dispelled. I've chosen to include research and excerpts from a number of both scientific and lay resources that help to complement and clarify what these women have shared. Although encouraged by the strides scientists and practitioners have made in the treatment of depression, I am not in the position of recommending any one course of treatment in this book, and will not use it to champion supposed "cures." I do, however, outline what these women find works best for them, describe in detail what it would take to replicate their steps to wellness, and spell out the exercises that they believe can make the most difference.

In my own experience, as well as the experience of many of the women I've talked to, it's the conversations that can do the most good. Helping each other come to grips with depression, its fallout, and the tools that help us all beat it back can be a lifesaving exercise. There is a good deal of evidence that shows connection with others generates optimism, is beneficial to our mental and physical health, and can help to drive a wedge against depression. That is why hearing from a multitude of women and gaining an understanding of the ins and outs of their own battles is so important. Without the language of science intervening, the truth is both easier to tell and to hear, and the feeling of connection is more easily had.

Along with the conversations, women found that there were certain ways of looking at themselves and their lives that needed to be actively changed before they got better. They talked with me and each other about what it was that really helped. I invite you to join this dialogue and, if you are currently depressed or hoping to inoculate yourself against future depressions, I encourage you to use this book to examine your own state. Follow the stories you identify with and let these women help you locate those aspects of your depression you want to work on. Then try to really answer the questions raised at the end of each chapter and take the time to try out the exercises in the last chapter. This book is designed to help you not only gain a sense of company and support but also have a look at how the topics covered relate to your personal experience of depression.

Feel free to take breaks as you read. If you are sensitive to depression or in the midst of one, too many of these stories at once could be overwhelming. Jump around if you'd like. If the earlier chapters are too "depressing," head to the back of the book where women tell how they control and overcome their depressions and arrive at a deeper appreciation of their lives. But most of all, remember that no matter how bad you can feel, depression ends, and when it does you'll have survived an ordeal that may well deepen you in unexpected ways. Every one of these women knows what it takes for them to get to the end, and in the following pages they are kind and brave enough to share their invaluable knowledge with the rest of us.

Chapter 1

Going Down

Depression can be an overwhelming amount of feeling, a too much, I'm-going-to-lose-my-mind sadness that doesn't let up. Or it can be a terrible emptiness. Then it feels more like a hollow sadness. It feels as if life around me is a movie, as if I'm watching some unreal thing that I'm not connected to, and the rest of the world is just this scenery that contains this cast of characters who are out there and functioning. They've got their denial working and their emotions in check and I'm laid up here in my house just watching. Completely immobilized.

—Leslie

I was ten years old when I had my first episode. My mother or my great-aunt, I can't remember which, had just thrashed me. The thrashings were always accompanied by yelling. I laid in my bed afterward, a bed I was still sharing with that same aunt, and felt a genuine despair.

—Grace

I don't think I would be where I am today if I had not been hospitalized. Hospitalization stripped away all of my freedoms. When you're stuck in a room and you can't even have a pair of shoes on with shoelaces in them, that really sends a message. At that point I made a conscious choice not to live in insanity.

—Gail

By the time I was able to distinguish the features of my most recent depression, I had already been in its grip for months. I was fighting typhoid fever in a southern Indian hospital when I first began to lose sleep. I stayed up for days, afraid if I slept the fever would gain the upper hand and kill me or I'd be subjected to the night terrors that had come in its wake. My panic attacks began then, as did questions about the meaning of my life, and the belief that the illness was punishment for a crime I was too shallow and worthless to recognize. When I got back to California a month later the bacteria was nearly gone but the insomnia and panic and self-hatred lived on, exacerbated by losing a lover and an important friend. For months I careened from doctor to doctor, assuming, in my own mind, the symptoms of various plausible illnesses related to the typhoid. I was certain there was a physical explanation for what was wrong with me. It felt purely physical. But as test after test found my body healthy, I had to finally recognize that what I was wasn't ill, but under the sway of a mood of the darkest hue, the very deepest blue.

So like a lot of women I know who've been overwhelmed by depression, for me there was a crash before there was an admission. In the smoldering aftermath of my crash I was able to discern when else in my life I had been crazy and what an absolute treasure the gift of denial can be. Denial and optimism had always been fast at my side before the crash. They abandoned me at the scene. In the this chapter we talk at length about what it feels like when denial fails and depression first hits. And how, after reaching out and attempting to steady ourselves, we might be able to go back to the scene and analyze the twists in the road that got us there.

When we look for clues about our depression, we're not always able to surmise a cause. What we learn instead are plot lines. We see the difficulties and disruptions, the old losses and the bad-for-you behaviors that form the clouds that stay heavy and dark overhead.

But whether it happens when we're four or fifty-four, for all of us there is an event, a day, a week or a year when we become *aware* of our depression. For many it's a slow dawning, a drag of time when the light of optimism starts to dim and then flash and finally pop, burning us into darkness. For others it's a rude shock. Perhaps it's the death of someone we love, or an unexpected health crisis, or the finality of a relationship's end that pitches our world into that darkness. However it hits, depression changes the world into a strangely brutal place, forcing us alone in the process. And as we navigate this lonely new night, encountering the monsters of disillusionment, physical and psychic pain, and consuming self-doubt, we learn that we are made up of more than happy thoughts, and vulnerable to the lasting nature of unexpressed sadness.

The Unreality of a First Episode

Whether we understand it as such when we're in the midst of an initial, tangible depressive episode, there is always a first time. Rita can still recall hers with perfect clarity. It all started sixteen years ago, the day her father died. "My dad died when I was fourteen, and up until then I had the normal teenage angst, questioning why people were so mean and judgmental, and I would stare at the sky and have really deep, dark teenager thoughts. When my father died, that changed. One day he was this handsome, healthy man and the next day he had cancer and was going to die in three to six months. And that's just what happened. I remember coming out of the funeral home. It was a sunny afternoon, a school day, and I looked across the street to see one of my classmates biking by, and I remember thinking I should be in school, and instead this weird thing was happening to me. I felt high, [as if] on drugs, and that feeling just stayed with me. I understood then that I was no longer a child and that people, including adults, can't handle death. I started doing drugs and drinking and no one did anything about it. The question became, how crazy can I act? It became clear that no one could handle my darkness. My depression became all-consuming. It stayed with me from that point until I was twenty-five. I used to think I just want to feel the way I felt before my dad died, but I couldn't go back. The wool had been taken off my eyes and I saw what the world was really like, a place where everything at any moment can just crash and it doesn't matter how safe and secure you think you are, it can all be taken away."

Gail, who is now in her mid-thirties, was in her early twenties when she hit bottom. "It was an unreciprocated relationship that set me off. I was having a really hard time dealing with the rejection and this woman's ambivalence, not knowing what she wanted from me or how to respond to her. The encounter led to therapy, which opened all these wounds. Eventually I tried to kill myself and landed in the hospital for a while. During that time and for about a year and a half afterward, I was chronically battling depression. I think that's the first time that I really ever realized that I wasn't just moody, that maybe there was a real, organic thing happening. My whole perspective on my moods changed. To this day the types of circumstances surrounding that relationship always throw me into a really edgy place."

Grace's first episode hit way back in the 1950s, when she was still a small child. It was a decade that found her too young and the culture too unaware to know what was happening. Now that she is in her fifties, Grace can see that her sad state of mind fit the circumstances. "I was ten years old when I had my first episode. My mother or my great aunt, I can't remember which, had just thrashed me. The thrashings were always accompanied by yelling. I laid in my bed afterward, a bed I was still sharing with that same aunt, and felt a genuine despair."

Although some of us, like Grace, have battled depression since childhood, others have thought themselves inured to it, and have made it well into adulthood before facing the feelings for the first time. It's not surprising. The average age of onset for women is twenty-seven. And though women of all ages get depressed, statistics show these depressions are most often concentrated between the ages of twenty-five and forty-four.

Leslie's experience of depression had always been of a kind of low-level self-hatred that would rise or fall, often depending on the state of her intimate relationships. Her depression became tangible after a bout with serious illness when she was thirty. "Even before I got sick there was an incident where a friend and I tried to save the lives of new-born puppies that had been strewn across a country road and left to die. Maybe we should have just left the puppies to their fate—they really were half dead already—but we wanted to try and save them so we went through these very emotional few days. When I was in the hospital my friend came and told me that despite our efforts all of the puppies were dead. At that point I was already out of my mind and wondering if I too was going to die. I reached this point of utter despair. My ideas about hope and good effort were getting squashed and the reality of our death-infused lives was echoed by all the suffering around me in the hospital, it was hitting me hard. Maybe it sounds dramatic, but so many of my illusions flew out those hospital windows and even when I was released and came home I couldn't get them back. It was like suddenly I was privy to the pain and the suffering in the world at large which served to magnify the long-ignored pain and suffering of my own life. I think what scared me the most was coming home, after I'd struggled so hard to live through the illness, and wanting to die. Everything just suddenly seemed like an enormous lie. All the people just part of some fiction, some movie. They were unaware, just as I had been before, of the sickening truth of life."

Mental health professionals cannot say with certainty what causes depression. Nor can many of the women I talked to. But some of them have had luck identifying their symptoms and managed to seek help early.

These women seem to know in the early stages of their initial depressions that they are drifting into danger-ous territory. A majority of us wait many months before we do the same. Terry, who is still recovering from the emotional and financial fallout of her last bout with depression, talks about reaching out for a diagnosis the first time, so that she could get treated right away. "The first time I was diagnosed it was with major depression and I didn't really care that much about the label. Whatever it took to get medication, whatever had to be on the form to ensure that I'd be given antidepressants was fine with me. The diagnosis was what it was, a means to an end to me at the time. I thought it was all situational. I had just come out of a relationship that was crazy and violent and I holed up in my college dorm room and didn't come out and didn't eat and didn't do anything but watch TV for days on end. Never took a shower. That's when you know something's wrong. When I could get up and function I went straight to the psychiatrist, thinking what I had was some sort of post-traumatic stress from the violent nature of the relationship."

There are others of us who experience a kind of depressive's amnesia surrounding our first tangible episode, and are sometimes also fuzzy on later episodes. We may have memories of our generally sad natures, or know that there was a kind of intervention taking place around us at the time of an episode, but precipitating factors can be lost to us. This often makes it harder to see a legitimate cause for the feelings that are arising prior to subsequent episodes and makes it easier to drift on down. Although Terry may have been clearheaded enough to get herself help the first time she went under, she doesn't remember whole chunks of the episode that has just passed and that landed her in the hospital, or much of the hospitalization for that matter. Emma remembers some of what contributed to the spotty episodes of depression that began for her in college, but is unclear on the specifics. "The first time it was suggested I go on medication was when I was in college. I've been sitting here trying to remember why and I can't remember, and the fact that I can't remember these things anymore gets me really depressed! I know that I was feeling excluded from friends because I had left school for a little while. But I know there was more to it than that. But the next time is clearer. I was in a bad car accident and had a head injury and afterward couldn't leave my house. Fear was the major emotion at the time. Since then, when I'm depressed, I'm not sure if it's because some fucked-up thing happened to my brain in the accident."

Mel remembers that her first intervention happened in high school, when her parents responded to her slipping grades, silence, and "unsuitable new friends" by sending her first to a school counselor and then to a therapist. She felt awful at the time but at that young age wasn't sure what was wrong. "You know, those years in high school, when depression hit for the first time, I don't think I remember breathing for that entire time. I know I must have been but I don't ever remember being able to take a really deep breath or really being able to see either. It was like I had been cloaked and blinded and couldn't feel more than a general sensation of atonal nothingness. I remember thinking, 'Wow, this is weird that this is life. I thought there was going to be more.' But all there was was just this flatline of emotion. When I look back I can see that my father was sick a lot then and angry, and my mother was mad or angry or sad, and I felt like I had to stay on the middle of that scale and couldn't afford to have any emotion. How could I? There was so much emotion swirling around me. So I started making friends with these kids who were from rougher families and I think I was drawn to them because, strangely, they seemed so much happier. I'm not sure if they truly were but they felt emotion, I can tell you that. It felt safer to me to be with them, to go on that roller-coaster of emotion and do some dangerous things. It felt safer to go someplace where there was feeling coming out of kids my age and get away from the vapid pool I'd go into at my house. My parents thought I was in danger though and so off I went to the therapist. They diagnosed me with severe depression then and put me on medication."

The Ways It Feels

We'll begin our lowdown on depression by examining how women report it really feels. As the study of depression becomes more and more advanced, the definition offered in the clinicians' bible, *The Diagnostic and Statistical Manual of Mental Disorders (DSM)*, broadens. The DSM considers depression to be made up of nine symptoms: a depressed mood; a diminished interest or pleasure in most activities; significant weight loss or weight gain that is unintentional, or a decrease or increase in appetite; insomnia or hypersomnia; psychomotor agitation or retardation; fatigue or loss of energy; feelings of worthlessness or excessive or inappropriate guilt; diminished ability to think or concentrate, or indecisiveness; and recurrent thoughts of death or suicide attempts. To be given a diagnosis of clinical depression, or what is called Major Depressive Episode, a person must show at least five of these symptoms, and one of those five must be depressed mood or diminished interest or pleasure. These symptoms must last for more than two weeks and not be a reaction to the death of a loved one or the onset of an organic disorder.

There are some common themes that emerge when women describe their own depressions. And though the differences of individual interpretation will come through, so will the compelling similarities. Some of these include the mode of detachment that you operate under in a depressive state and the deadening of hope and purpose that immobilizes you. There's the way the world around you seems to be part overwhelming reality, part movie set façade. There are the strange new eating and sleeping habits, and the thoughts of suicide. And then there's the way you can feel so empty and at the same time so flowing-over full of sadness and dread.

Sadness and Helplessness

Anne says, "With depression all feels hopeless and helpless. It's hard for me to concentrate on any one thing for even a short period of time, which in turn makes me very upset with myself for not doing things. It comes on slowly, like drops of water from a faucet that gradually fill your body until you are saturated with feelings of sadness and worthlessness. Inevitably I become a recluse, sleep excessively, cry and cry."

Detachment and Emptiness

Rita talked a lot in her interview about the mode of detachment she operated under after her dad's death. She fed this disconnection with drugs and alcohol, attempting in vain to sink the immovable depression that had taken hold. She did succeed in keeping it at bay, for a while. "Let me tell you about feeling empty. After my father passed there was nothing inside of me. When I was a teenager I was loaded every day and that helped, that was great. People didn't think I had a problem. My psychiatrist, who I paid a hundred dollars an hour, didn't think I had a problem, but it's because I looked good and I went to school and I knew how to bullshit. I drank, did pot, coke, speed, anything I could get my hands on. One day when I was riding to see my father in the hospital I made a conscious choice. I was a pretty straight kid and I said out loud to my older brother, who was driving us, I cannot handle this reality, give me drugs please. And he did. I think the drugs saved me because the experience I had at that age would've sent me over the edge. What happened was eventually the numbing effect of the drugs stopped working. I would drink and drink and drink and do more and more drugs and feel the same. That is fucking scary, sitting there and realizing, 'Oh my god, it's not working.' The first thing that comes is fear of suicide. I was already hurting myself at the time. I wasn't ready to kill myself but I was locking myself in the bathroom and making myself bleed and spreading blood all around and getting in that, I don't know if you've been there, but that psychotic place and knowing it. Thinking, 'Whew! I am really crazy! I'm over the edge!'"

Overwhelm of Feeling and Deadening of Hope and Purpose

For Carol the depression she experienced thirty-five years ago materialized as a strong sense of "isolation and feeling 'boxed-in' or trapped by the feelings of powerless-ness and hopelessness and unhappiness. I felt as if these feelings would never leave, as is they'd become a perma-nent part of me. It got difficult to be around others. Fam-ily, friends, strangers—it made no difference, they were all too far away. I had a total loss of energy and normal work or home activities became impossible. All of my energy and concentration were focused on the feelings of being depressed. I had had lows before and have had them since, but found that nothing compares to real depression."

Kitty, who is in her thirties, has cycled in and out of depression since she was a teenager. "I've had about five or six major episodes starting when I was sixteen. There didn't appear to be a pattern of any kind except that most of them happened in the winter. For a few of them there was an every-two-years pattern, but I broke that this year. They usually last two months. At least eight weeks, and sometimes more. Only one wasn't in the winter. It differs from how I feel the rest of the time because it feels like I'm dead instead of alive. Everything just feels empty and flat and nothing can have a good outcome and I stop eating and sleeping and I cry all the time. I withdraw from every-one in my life. I always have to rebuild my social life after I have a depression.

"Depression is an existential thing for me. It's a spiri-tual crisis where nothing seems to have any meaning. So I just stop feeding anything in my life and literally myself by not eating. It's like I have no appetite. The content of my depression has never been, 'Oh I can't get a man,' it's always, 'What's the point?' Always."

Changes in Eating and Sleeping Patterns

Brenda pigs out and sleeps when she's depressed. "I gorge on food. Especially chocolate chips. When I am depressed I'll eat entire bags of chocolate chips and sleep whenever possible."

Grace reacts similarly. "My depression feels like a damp, deep, dark cave. I feel weak, victimized, and nonproductive when it hits. I retreat or end up hiding out. I eat food I wouldn't normally eat, like McDonald's apple pies. And I overeat—tons of potato chips and chocolate. I fail to exercise, stop reading. I watch television and read *People* magazine."

June, who has soothed her long-standing depression with drugs for years, is now trying to get clean. She's finding that her depression is still with her, sometimes even stronger than before since the drugs aren't around to medicate it. Her depression takes a form that is familiar to many. She has those telltale problems with sleep. "Sometimes I can't get up; other times I haven't been going to my program because I'm trying to sleep it all away. But when I wake up it's still there and it doesn't go away. It's more compounded every day. I sleep because I don't even want to deal with it. I feel like if I sleep and my family members leave then I won't have to hear their mouth, I don't have to hear the reminder of why I'm where I am or what my plight is. Sometimes I try to get into the TV and I can't even watch it. Sometimes I'm just lying here awake or asleep. It's not that I don't want to get up and help myself. That's not it. That's not what it's about. I don't know. There is so much going on. And what happens a lot of times is that I lie awake at night and that's why I'm asleep during the day. At night I can't sleep because I'm stressing about the whole situation."

Dreams of Death

Mel's suicidal feelings were there from her first experience with depression. "I had certainly thought about suicide in high school but I think that that can sometimes be a normal high school, angst thing. Plus I didn't pursue it very far because there was so much other drama going on that I had enough of it to play with. So by the time I got to college, and I'm not sure what set this in motion, but I remember being very aware that I had the means to take my own life and that if I were to walk back in to my dorm room I would do that. I remember on particular nights having actual moments where I'd be standing at the door of my room and I knew if I walked through it I could take an overdose of some prescription drugs I had and they would put me to sleep and I would be dead. That's when I started to scare myself, and it was odd, but it was right around the time that I was starting to experience some life. So I made these conscious decisions to turn away from the door with my brain telling me that I should hold on and see what's here. My life was changing."

Grace just kind of stops when her depression hits, and the suicidal feelings are a familiar part of this stopping. "I've always had daily suicidal feelings. It's better now but I once saw suicide as a friend and a seducer. I figured it would just be a matter of time before I was successful at it, and in my twenties I made a number of attempts. I used to admire those people who had killed themselves: Sylvia Plath, Hemingway, Kurt Cobain."

Kitty has thought about suicide a lot, but losing a good friend to it helped her to shift her perspective. "With suicide, I end up in this trap. My best friend suffered from depression and she killed herself. My friend did a decent job but I would blow it. My friend never screwed up anything in her life. Everything she did she executed beautifully, including her own death. I went on a retreat because it was either that or drive my car off a cliff. Anyway, I know it wouldn't be perfect and painless for me. I'm such a bumbler. Ultimately what she did was just so hard on people who were left behind."

It's important to take suicidal feelings seriously. They are a definite sign that it is time to get help for your depression. Fifteen percent of chronic depression cases end in suicide. The devastating reality of this statistic is made all the worse when we realize that nearly 90 percent of all cases of depression can be effectively treated.

Exhaustion

Thankfully, most women say, depressive symptoms wax and wane over time. You need only be depressed for two weeks to receive a diagnosis of Major Depressive Episode. One of the hallmarks of depression is that it occurs cyclically; it is truly rare for symptoms to be constant. Nevertheless, it doesn't take long for a depressed woman to be exhausted by the depression. Or, conversely, for an exhausted woman to begin to show signs of depression.

Brenda's postpartum depression was one of the hardest periods in her life. "When I gave birth to my second child, I already had another—a soon-to-be three-year-old who was active and had daily temper tantrums. I was overwhelmed to say the least. I was breastfeeding my son around the clock, being up at night with him, and then up during the day with my daughter. It was exhausting. By the time my son was three to four months old, I was depressed. It was as if my body, mind, and soul were all tired. I was lonely and frustrated and wondering if I would ever feel like myself again. The days were so long and my husband and I were completely disconnected. When we went to counseling they diagnosed me as depressed. I was. I felt like I was alone on a dead-end street."

Uncovering a Prior Record

Many of the women felt that the experience of their first episode released a watershed of memories and insight into the past. Women who are plagued with depressed feelings in childhood or adolescence often attribute them in later life to the normal pains of growing up. But once you've had a major depressive episode, you're inclined to revisit this idea. Suddenly low affect and strange behavior in your early years seem to take on new meaning. You start to wonder, "Could the seeds of what's happening now have been planted so early in my life?" "Could really investigating and clarifying earlier depressions help to guard against future tumbles?"

Screenwriter Kendall says, "I didn't even know that I had been depressed until I was really depressed and then I realized I've been depressed a lot of different times in my life. I was finally diagnosed with clinical depression in

1996, but when the diagnosis came down, I was shocked to realize I had felt this way before—when I was eight, and probably when I was two. I just couldn't put a name on it before. I can remember now that when I was eight I kept getting sick and I couldn't go to school and my mom took me to the doctor, and he kept saying nothing was wrong with me. We took all of these tests anyway because my stomach hurt all the time and blood vessels were popping in my eyes. When I think back on it I know the broken blood vessels and the persistent redness around my eyes were from crying all the time."

Kendall's friend Cherise concurs. "I'd never thought that I had been depressed when I was younger. I always just imagined that that was my reality. When I started reading journals that I'd kept as a teenager, that's when it dawned on me. The pages were filled with things like 'Mom wants to kill herself today,' and 'I feel really sad and want to slice my body with a knife.' You don't realize at that point in your life that that's not what everyone else is going through. You don't put a name to it."

Meninger Clinic psychologist Dr. Harriet Lerner (1989), an expert in the psychology of women, has specu- lated that we begin to experience depression when we compromise our wants and needs and thereby lose a part of ourselves. This usually happens for the first time in fam- ilies of origin, when girls learn what can sometimes be an excessive amount of self-sacrifice. They do this when "too much of the self (one's beliefs, values, wants, priorities, ambitions) becomes negotiable under relationship pres- sures" (201).

Terry knows that her depression was born early, and thinks it was partly affected by the intense fighting that went on between her parents, which she learned to accommodate by disappearing. "I don't think that I had identifiable bouts of melancholy that people could look at and say: 'She's depressed.' But my family life consisted of a lot of rage, violence, screaming. When people screamed in my family they would get so out of control that they'd make noises like animals. I would just lock myself in my room and click off. When I was growing up I was numb and felt like I was watching a movie happen around me. That I wasn't connected to myself but watching myself interact with other people who are like characters on a screen. At that point it feels like it's not really you. I felt very disconnected and I think that was just a big protection mechanism. I remember my brother used to say, 'You have no feelings. The only time you cry is when you're watching TV.' And he was right, that was the only time I would emote. For me depression is all about repressed anger and not having a voice. Expectations are put on you that you cannot meet and so you just say 'fuck it' and zone out. There would be points when I would be almost comatose, staring at the walls after one of those family fights. They'd have the kind of fights where if you hear any more, you're just going to flip out. You are going to go to the hospital. You're almost sure you're going to die. So I got very good at clicking off and zoning. Later, when I actually started to feel things, when I fell in love for the first time, it was like a floodgate had opened."

Grace also traces her depression back to her younger days, admitting that it wasn't until she went on antidepressants in her forties that she "finally understood why most people got such joy out of life. I believe that I had clinical depression, that in my case the depression became an integral part of my personality. I always suffered some form of daily, low-grade depression."

Down and Down Again

There are differing schools of thought on the "repeatability" of depression in women's lives. Statistics warn that half of all women who have a major depressive episode experience at least one more in their lifetime. The good news is that if depression makes its way back, we will at least have had the previous experience to learn from and build on, and we'll recognize it earlier. We will also know, like the countless others do, that the feelings will eventually lift.

Soon after newscaster Mike Wallace came forward with his depression, Kathy Cronkite interviewed him for her book, *On the Edge of Darkness* (1994). He described two depressive episodes and said, "What can you do? Patience, listen, reassure, reassure. You look at a scratch on your hand, you know it's going to heal; *you know.* Why do you know? Because you've seen it so many times. Little by little it heals; it knits, and it's better. Maybe it leaves a bit of a scar. So you take that on faith. I'm saying, do the same with the soul, or the head, or the mind, or the spirit, or whatever it is. It is going to get better" (20). As all of the women attest, it is important to remember the eventual healing when you encounter those once-baffling feelings and symptoms for a second time.

Kitty's been there six times. When it starts out, she says, she feels it "physiologically. It just feels like a heaviness. And then I gradually notice my thoughts changing.

Usually there are both negative thoughts in my head and positive thoughts. And the way I experience depression is the positive voices get quieter and quieter and quieter until I can't hear them anymore, and it's like none of those ideas exist anymore. It's a dying out of anything positive or optimistic. But at first it's just a little bit less and then a little bit less. It's gradual."

Leslie sees it a couple of ways. "For me depression can be an overwhelming amount of feeling, a too-much, I'm-going-to-lose-my-mind sadness that doesn't let up, or it can be a terrible emptiness. Then it's more of a hollow sadness. It feels as if life around me is a movie, as if I'm watching some unreal thing that I'm not connected to, and the rest of the world is just this scenery that contains this cast of characters who are out there and functioning. They've got their denial working and their emotions in check and I'm laid up here in my house just watching. Completely immobilized. I know it's starting to end when I want to be mobile again. But each time the feeling is deeply painful."

For Mel, the initial "emotional flatlining" she experienced in high school came back strong in and after college, but has lessened in severity now that she's crowding forty. "The depression came back in college but that time I didn't get medicated for it. I knew that I was going through another period like I had before. I recognized the signs, and I sought out the psychologist I had seen as a kid and talked to her for a really long time. I got the sense from her that the questioning was an important part of getting better. This was after becoming monosyllabic again."

For Kendall it's a rise in anger. "I think the thing that I notice the most when I'm depressed that just isn't there when I'm feeling better is that I'm incredibly angry. I get so angry I don't even know what to do with myself. Like yesterday at work someone said something to me and I banged my fist on the desk. I feel like I could smash things, throw things against the window. I feel like I could hurl my body against broken glass and it would feel great. I just wanna fuck things up really bad. And I want to hurt other people. I feel like I could. Like control could just easily elude me.

"I'm having a hard time with my depression right now and when the anger comes out it's not so much that I feel like I'm empty, but I do feel disconnected. My biggest priority in life is to be connected, and I work at my relationships really hard, my marriage and my friends and my family—even my fucked-up family—so when I get depressed and feel really disconnected, I notice it. Today I feel disconnected from my son, who is the light of my life and my closest relationship. I was so mad at him today because he was acting out, and I'm sure that he picked up on how fucked up I was. He was picking up CDs and throwing them on the floor. And I was saying, 'Would you stop that?' and at a certain point I was yanking him away from the CD shelf and I felt like I could've hit him. And I've never thought I could hit my kid but that's how disconnected I feel, not only from my kid but from myself as a parent and myself as me."

Gail's depression has returned a number of times since her hospitalization twelve years ago. But she maintains that after each episode she's gotten a little wiser: "When I'm in it, I feel like my perspective is shot, like my world has collapsed and the sum total of my life and experience has been reduced to this moment of feeling. And there's a sense now of 'Fuck, here we go again.' I've just resigned myself when it starts to come in to allow it to run its course. I think it was three weeks ago Monday that I couldn't get up. I had to call in sick and resign myself to it. I think the first time is the worst. For me it translated into hospitalization. Total breakdown. Total psychic and physical and psychological breakdown and I don't know that I will ever experience it to that degree again."

Summary Questions:
How do you go down?

A few of the women interviewed, especially those who had not spent a lot of time dealing with the mental health system, were still unclear about what depression is "supposed" to feel like. Their descriptions were of symptoms that certainly conjured a genuine depressive experience, but maybe they weren't sleeping a lot, like their diagnosed friend had, or were furious all the time and concerned that their problem was one of anger, not depression. To not know if you are experiencing a "legitimate" depression is a common experience. The majority of people with depression are never diagnosed and a full two-thirds never receive treatment.

Consider what you've read so far, how you would classify your own feelings, and where you might fit into this dialogue. Get a piece of paper and a pen, then use the following questions as a prompt to describe your own depression.

❖ What does it feel like?

❖ How does your life change? What do you start doing more or less of?

❖ When does it come on?

❖ Can you go back in time and think of other episodes? Do they feel the same as your most recent or current episode(s)?

❖ Can you remember what may have triggered those early episodes?

❖ Now describe how you feel when you are not depressed.

❖ Can you remember what helped you get out of your past depressions? Can you imagine what could help you now?

❖ What about your experience was similar to what these women had to say? Does or did anything from your experience seem different?

❖ If you were feeling isolated in your depression, did knowing that so many women have gone through depression change that at all?

❖ Which of your own depressive symptoms are most disturbing to you? If you were to choose one to work on, one that might have a ripple effect on your other symptoms, which one would it be?

Chapter 2

The Deeper the Depth

When I came out of my depression I felt like I had to completely reconstruct my value structure. I think that's a really crucial part of it. Finding some kind of understanding with yourself and the world. For me the key to moving through depression has been coming to some sort of understanding of the mystery of life. Depression is a catalyst for clarity.

—Gail

I had these romantic ideas about depression. Ideas that it was spiritually important or made you a better person or more artistic. That there was something fulfilling about it. I was not prepared for how crazy it made me feel. How I wasn't going to be able to go outside my door. The romance is gone for me.

—Leslie

I always feel that I've deepened after a depression. It's like 'Oh, there's so much to be alive about now that I've been dead for eight weeks, twelve weeks, longer.' I think it makes me more compassionate. To contemplate suffering is a spiritual act. In connection to how other people are suffering it's often hard to hold on to compassion. It's hard to stay in touch with your own. That's why we're so mean to suffering people, because they are reminding us of our suffering. Of our guilt.

—Kitty

In northern California where I live, there is a constant threat of wildfires during the dry seasons. If you drive down rural highways or up steep hill roads you find signs that gauge fire risk dotting the roadsides. Local newscasts regularly feature interviews with shell-shocked families standing before smoldering backlots of rubble that were once their homes. I can still see one middle-aged man with a crew cut and a neatly trimmed mustache, telling a reporter that he never could empathize with people who lost everything to a disaster until he became one of them. He then looked directly at the reporter as if he wanted to go on, but paused and shook his head and looked away. You watched him realize right then that he couldn't explain his pain in sound bites.

In her book of interviews with celebrities with depression, Walter Cronkite's daughter Kathy (1994) draws a distinction between the colloquial use of the term depression and the kind of depression that she and her interviewees have experienced. "One of the great misunderstandings people have about clinical, or medical, depression stems from the colloquial sense of the word to mean less than happy," Cronkite says. "To some, 'depression' can sound ordinary, inconsequential" (21). And when there is such confusion, a short pep talk or a nicely placed platitude may seem to the person who is not depressed like a solid comfort. But it may be that truly understanding depression is only possible through the experience of it. It often means becoming the man who lost his house. Getting to this place requires a depth of suffering uncommon to many daily lives. It makes platitudes and sound bites obsolete.

I for one had always fed on platitudes. They were perfect for someone like me who liked the tangible and actively resisted drifting around too much in my mind. I may have understood that there are both dark recesses and airy places of beauty in our psyches, and that exploring them could add some depth to my existence, but with little of the existential curiosity I'd seen in others I also thought I was coasting along just fine. Life was to be sensed, laughed at, or at the very worst navigated. To stop and ponder it was an altogether unfamiliar idea, even in times of trouble. Probably most especially then.

Oddly enough, when I was at my most depressed, backing away from my fissuring mind and turning toward old solid distracting comforts started to seem like a perverse and unacceptable action. To suddenly be there, at this crazy place I had actively avoided so hard for so long, seemed terribly meaningful. And no matter anyway, there was no way that I could break free. I was, like all of us whimpering in the steel-toothed grip of an episode, utterly caught in my head.

Loved ones who'd never been where I was would try to loosen me then with profundity. But they rarely did better than "What doesn't kill you only makes you stronger," and "Time heals all wounds." Suddenly these grave old phrases came across like dime-store versions of the truth, and started sounding like the dreary commands I was used to from a childhood of catechism. They didn't help, and more often than not, just made me feel cheated. The thing that well people don't always get is that depression often means something to the depressive. And it's usually something less pithy than a platitude.

"I guess I just felt that when the bad lows hit they wouldn't be as bad as they are," says Leslie. "With depression, I don't know, I had this romantic idea that yes it would be tough but it would also be really powerful. It would change me into something real. Like physical illness or a new disability seems to do to all of those testimonial-making people out there. I didn't expect to feel like I wanted to die. I didn't expect to feel like the world was a lie. I didn't expect to feel like nothing mattered anymore. I didn't expect to feel like I couldn't get it up for any of my friends. I guess I just thought it would bring me insight. I think we dismiss depression in this culture to be something less difficult than it is. Nothing prepared me for what it was really like. When other people would try to comfort me with those stock words of wisdom, they just seemed shallow and useless."

The Soul of It

When it comes down to decoding the real meaning of depression, women are all over the map. There are those of us who see it as a great teacher, leading us deeper into the thickets of life's truths. Others find it to be an important leveler that helps us better understand the human condition and our own compassionate place within it. But some, like Leslie, still think it's too high a price to pay for a little wisdom. And others, like Kendall, think that it's sometimes just a big, biochemical trick.

"I think that your mind tricks you into thinking this is reality because nothing feels as real as depression does. I don't think that's real. I think your biochemistry is fucked up and your serotonin is not getting where it's supposed to be and it's not necessarily real. I think that there's this belief that when you're depressed you're at your most realistic. I'm sorry, but that's bullshit.

"I was going through postpartum depression and every story about dead kids on the TV just slayed me, and every time I walked toward the window with my infant in my arms I would imagine what would happen if he fell out the window. There was constant pressure on my brain to make what was going on with me, which was so beautiful, into this terrible thing. And that was the depression. It was distorting the reality of my life. The reality is I'm not gonna throw my baby out the window and the reality is he's probably not gonna die at the hands of a gang member. That to me is the experience of depression. If you're depressed you can be sensitized to all the pain and suffering in the world and you're stripped of all your coping mechanisms. I could tell you the story of the dead kids and you're not left crying. So what is real? What is objective reality? It certainly isn't depression."

Here in the Western world, depression is a problem in need of solving. In other parts of the world, it is a normal and accepted part of life. And in the East, in cultures that have been influenced by Buddhist and Hindu teachings, it could be construed as the first step to enlightenment. Funnily enough, this sample of women seems, by turns, to agree with all three interpretations.

Anne is a spiritual person. She wasn't so spiritual before her depression hit. But she also contends that it's not necessarily the depression that brought her her spirituality. "Depression is a silent enemy. It is not tangible and it is very difficult to understand. It gradually takes over your life in small increments until you are almost totally consumed with thoughts of helplessness, hopelessness, worthlessness. You become full of anxiety and restlessness with no point of reference or clear perception of where you are going. Goal setting becomes impossible. I don't feel that there was any spirituality in my depression, nor did it cause any feelings of spirituality once it was conquered."

Sharon feels similarly, although she also sees an inherent relationship: Her spirituality is the strength that gets her through her depressions. "There are big differences between being depressed sometimes—who isn't—and the level of depression I experience these days, which can last for months and months and makes it almost impossible to do anything. If I did not have a strong spiritual search and experience much finer forces than the ones that govern one's life when one is depressed, I would be dead or institutionalized by now. There are times I lose all hope but the finer forces still seem to support me. When you have depression short term it helps you question things and can be a spiritual experience. When it is at the level called clinical depression I do not find it so spiritual. For the first six months after my hysterectomy I studied my depression with my whole spiritual arsenal. I learned where it lived in me, how it felt, what prompted it, etc. Now, five years later, it is rarely so interesting. Mostly I want it to end. However, I will say that as a consequence I have gone back to school at fifty-two to study traditional healing and have been getting traditional treatments, which seem to be slowly building something new inside. But this rebuilding is a very, very new thing and I have been disappointed before.

"Depression itself is as easily a hindrance as a help to spirituality. If it is a part of one's path and one knows it, then it does not matter what it is, it helps. Without a path, well, it may be what moves one to look or it may be what stops one's journey. There is no one answer."

Other women do feel that depression is linked in some way to the soul, and that the awful feelings they've sustained in a depressive state have legitimate meaning.

Rita is one. "I honestly feel like you can't be happy without pain. You can't see light without dark. I really feel like you need the contrast and I feel like in my life, I will always want to help people, and how can you help someone if you haven't experienced what they're going through? I think depression is very valuable. I'm glad that I've had it and all the experiences that I've had. All the pain and all the bullshit has been totally enriching."

Gail makes an even more direct connection between her depression and her spirituality. "There's a Buddhist saying that to be a vessel is to be empty. That place of complete and total emptiness has always brought the question of, 'What am I alive for?' But I had to be completely empty in order to come back to the real true euphoria of life. It always follows those periods of total emptiness. And sometimes it is induced by loneliness. I think lately it's more induced by that than anything else. But then at the moment of total emptiness the phone rings or I hook up with a friend and I remember and my perspective shifts. I think that there's a real benefit to that point in depression and unfortunately I think a lot of the philosophy behind treating depression is that it's a disease and we can make you better. I don't think it's a disease, I think it's part of the life experience. I think everybody should experience that part of the life experience. And everybody eventually does. Everybody experiences that complete and total realization that you do probably at infancy, that you are completely alone in the world. And, ultimately, you are."

Gail and many of the women are quick to say that these insights came to them toward the end of episodes. It is not depression per se, but the mindfulness that arises out of dealing with the depression that has the potential to alter and ultimately heal.

Mel says, "I think depression is mostly a signal to me now, whereas when I was younger it didn't signal anything to me, it just was. I had no control over it. I don't think I necessarily have control over it now. But when I find myself not breathing in the world, not stepped into my own body, like the world is happening to me, or when I feel no emotion or feel unplugged from emotion, it's a good signal for me to step back and take a huge breath and try to figure out where I need to make a move. So it feels like a huge spiritual road sign. One that reads, 'Isn't there someplace else you'd rather be?'"

Kitty says it's the end of a depression that enriches her. "I always feel that I've deepened after a depression. It's like, 'Oh, there's so much to be alive about now that I've been dead for eight weeks, twelve weeks, longer.' I think it makes me more compassionate. To contemplate suffering, is a spiritual act. In connection to how other people are suffering it's often hard to hold on to compassion. It's hard to stay in touch with your own. That's why we're so mean to suffering people, because they are reminding us of our suffering. Of our guilt."

The Spirit of the East

When I was at my suicidal worst, one of my dearest friends sent me a tape by a female Tibetan monk who contended that falling into despair was nothing to be concerned about. She taught that we in the West are consumed with keeping despair at bay, but that "lows" are an inevitable and important part of living. In fact they can sometimes be one of the only ways we Westerners are able to rest. She had noticed that physical illness was one of our only forms of meditation: one of the only times we both give ourselves a break, and are left to contemplate our troubles and our blessings. Depression could be another. Her words struck me as radical, and were a strong contrast to the worried rush of action undertaken by the Western therapists and doctors around me.

Cross-cultural studies have confirmed that people all over the world are faced with depression, and that women indeed do suffer at higher rates than men, wherever they live. The cultural differences arise when it comes to conceptualizing the depressive state and the relative rate of alarm it evokes in the sufferers and their caretakers. Many of the women I spoke with (and they were all, whatever their racial or cultural makeup, raised at least since childhood here in the States), used the words "emptiness" and "disconnection" to describe their state. They were anxious to feel "full" and "connected" again. The striking thing about their chosen words is that in many Eastern religious traditions, "emptiness" and "disconnection" are states that one aspires to. They are instrumental in achieving enlightenment. They, to put it bluntly, are good for you.

These kinds of ideas are difficult for some of us to accept. I, for one, had a good friend quietly kill himself after falling into yet another "deepened" state. But I am willing to consider that there may be something to be said about the context in which he fell apart. Would it have gone differently if he'd been raised to believe that his pain was normal, acceptable, even important? How did his culture and its beliefs support or abandon him during his darkest hours?

In his best-selling book, *Going to Pieces Without Falling Apart*, psychotherapist and practicing Buddhist Dr. Mark Epstein (1998) draws on the hidden similarities of therapy and Buddhist practice to illustrate the rather tight way in which we in the West try to keep ourselves together. Both psychotherapy and Buddhism seek to help us understand how and why our defenses don't always work. Often people enter therapy hoping to further tighten and strengthen their defenses but eventually learn that this tightness often brings us more pain and drives us farther from liberating truths about life, death, and creativity. There are times when therapists may encourage their clients' experiences of dissolution, but more often they will help them become versed in techniques that lift them out of that state and secure them in thoughts and feelings of happiness again. However, the most often prescribed and successful therapy used to deal with depression today is something called CBT or "cognitive-behavioral therapy." It does nothing short of help clients change their thought patterns by teaching them techniques like "thought stopping," where a depressing or compulsively negative thought is shooed out of the mind to make room for more positive or neutral thought patterns. In some small way, by encouraging us to step back from the useless racket that is negative thinking, CBT helps us to achieve a deeper sense of the quiet inherent in all of us, and helps us recognize and let go of our depressive rattlings. This kind of result is a defining principle in many forms of Eastern meditation.

As distinct from therapy, some theorize that Western psychological traditions themselves, with their encouragement of separateness and individuation, help to contribute to the weight of the depressive experience. These traditions lead us to believe that when we're down, we're even further devoid of the kind of power and strength and insight that lead to that pinnacle of mental health, true Western independence. Epstein says, "Psychology has been suspicious of the wisdom traditions of the world's great religions because these traditions have preserved a capacity of the self that Western psychology has all but whited out . . . the melting of the ego has been seen as something that only babies or crazy people do with any regularity. . . . Rather than seeing the self as an expanding and contracting, coalescing and dissolving, separating and merging organism, Western psychology views the self as something that has to be developed or improved throughout its one-way journey toward separateness" (84–85).

Kitty describes a time in her life when the Western and Eastern approaches came up against each other. "When I went into the hospital I had bottomed. For me, heading in there was realizing that it was up to me. No one could help me but myself—no one could. My family said, 'Go in for a little while,' and my boyfriend couldn't deal with me because I was crying and not eating. He was going nuts and missing work and losing sleep and he couldn't take care of me anymore. So the only other choice was going to my parents' house again and I thought, uh-uh. But once I was in the hospital I felt like I was in this netherworld. They were trying me on these new drugs, and then told me if I left the hospital without permission I wouldn't have anyone to give me my drugs. While you're in there you sit around and they want to talk with you about current events. They have current events, and arts and crafts. Some people seem to like it there. Some people who were there told me they checked themselves in regularly. The staff kept threatening me with 'If you leave too soon you're going to end up back here.' So there's this psychological trap of disempowerment. It's 'you don't know what you need, I know what you need.' There was a guy there that I'd see for ten minutes once every couple of days and I had to do my best with him because he was my ticket out. I told this guy that my issue was that I don't have a sure enough sense of identity, of where I end and the world begins. His suggestion was to try me on an antipsychotic drug. He justified it by saying people have reported that they've felt more of a sense of self on the drug. That's so far-fetched and implausible! They'll just try anything. The funniest people in there were the people who had been on every medication in the world and they'd sit on couches and list them off: 'Oh, I got hives on that one and on that other one my shit turned green.'

"When I got out of the hospital I went to a spiritual retreat in the desert and all the people there helped me. I really believe that for me depression is a spiritual crisis with existential content. I went from a place that had no spiritual orientation to a place that knew exactly what I needed and I was helped and benefited from that. If only the cultural context in the West weren't to try to medicate depression into oblivion, and weren't to label and isolate. If the whole cultural context had shifted, then maybe it could be an enriching experience. When people go sit in vipasana for twelve days or three months or a year they dwell in some pretty shitty things; they ruminate. And if we switched the context of it, maybe depression would be seen as more spiritual. It's all about what we think about it."

My Cross to Bear

Many women also assign meaning to depression by way of Christian religion. Judy, mother of five, says, "I have very strong religious beliefs, among them that life is sacred. I think that there is a spiritual component to having endured depression. I truly felt at the time that it was my Gethsemane, my cross to bear." The Bible is rife with stories about surviving through suffering but then also draws a direct correlation between suffering and sin. There are times when this latter connection can worsen a woman's depression, can encourage her to stay in a depressed state and accept it as punishment. But because of the religious meaning Christian women can find in suffering, they are also often able to justify surviving it. They have learned that on the other side of pain is redemption.

Kathy Cronkite (1994) quotes psychologist Betty Sue Flowers on this topic. Flowers says, "[What is happening to] someone who said they were having a spiritual crisis, a dark night of the soul, and someone who said 'I'm an atheist, I'm just having a physiological depression' [is probably the same] electrochemically, but it would be experienced differently. In the dark night of the soul, although all hope is lost and you feel completely disconnected from God, you have a larger framework in which to put that; it's not like just being in a pit. You may cry, 'My God, my God, why hast Thou forsaken me?' but there is the understanding of a story in which that has happened. In the old days people used to say, 'I'm being tested by God.' Put in that context, it's a meaningful experience. If it's just depression, it's a meaningless experience, which adds to the depression, and then why bother existing?" (205).

Cronkite also quotes an agreeing William Styron, who says, "I do recall reading Job when I was able to concentrate, rather avidly reading Job. I realized that, as I had been told, this is very likely his expression of what it was like to be suffering from depression. And if he got through it, I could get through it. So to that extent there was . . . a sense that if I could get through this there must be some sort of redemption of myself involved" (209).

Blue Creatives

Exploring the meaning of depression has long been the domain of artists, musicians, poets, and writers. The arts afford both the artist and the public an acceptable arena for this exploration. There is a common speculation that artists have more personal experience with depression than the general public, when the truth is people of all backgrounds and interests suffer. Still, out of these ideas come the assumptions not only that creative people are fated to experience depression, but also that anyone who has experienced depression may have grown creatively.

Actress Winona Ryder, who brought Susanna Kaysen's *Girl, Interrupted* (a funny and poignant book about a young woman's institutionalization) to the big screen, has spoken frankly about her own hospital stay, her numerous depressive episodes, and the relationship between her depression and art. It is a relationship that she always saw as vital. "I thought [depression] made me a better actress," she's said. "It's part of what makes us human . . . it's what makes me want to act . . . it's exploring both sides." She describes a "piercing loneliness" that accompanied her depressions—something that many creative and depressed people can easily identify with.

Mark Epstein furthers the connection between emptiness and insight when he mentions the work of D. W. Winnicott. A Freudian, Winnicott believed that many of our emotional problems stemmed from the developmental problems with separateness that we have as children. In his mind, the inability to accept the bad in the good parent stunts our natural ability to experience both closeness and separation. Hence the pain associated with loneliness. The simultaneous experience of closeness and separation does exist: It can be found in the infant/mother dynamic and in the lingering moments after sex, when a kind of "floating" is permitted. "This kind of aloneness," proposed Winnicott, "is the foundation of all creativity, since it is only in such a state that it is possible to explore one's internal world" (38–39).

The kind of aloneness that depression promotes in many people is often seen as the most fertile ground for creative growth. This is a decidedly different separateness than occurs in the Western ideal of independence, which requires an active effort to wall off feeling, and is accompanied by a pride in the strength required to face life's challenges alone. These distinctions about creative versus American aloneness fuel the arguments about the good of suffering and the supposed relationship between a painful aloneness and creativity. It is one thing to learn to be strong and alone, but something unacceptable to be feeling strongly while alone. It is what has some people crying foul about the potent possibilities of psychoactive drugs that can bland down the painful emotions that are at times associated with creative growth. Why encourage the healing of depression by Western standards, when it could bring about the death of creativity?

Dr. Kay Redfield Jamison (1993), a psychiatrist known for books about her own and others' manic depression, takes on this question in an involving analysis of the artistic temperament called *Touched with Fire*. Although concentrating on artists, writers, poets, and musicians who suffered primarily from bipolar illness, she does consider unipolar depression and the greater question of the link between mental illness and creativity at large.

"There must be serious concern about any attempt to reduce what is beautiful and original to a clinical syndrome, genetic flaw, or predictable temperament," writes Jamison. "It is frightening, and ultimately terribly boring, to think of anyone—certainly not only writers, artists, and musicians—in such a limited way. The fear that medicine and science will take away from the ineffability of it all, or detract from the mind's labyrinthian complexity, is as old as man's attempts to chart the movement of the stars. Even John Keats, who had studied to be a surgeon, felt that

Newton's calculations would blanch the heavens of their glory. The natural sciences, he wrote, 'will clip an Angel's wings,/ conquer all mysteries by rule and line./ Empty the haunted air, and gnomed mine—/Unweave a rainbow.'" Jamison goes on to say that "What remains troubling is whether we have diminished the most extraordinary among us—our writers, artists, and composers—by discussing them in terms of psychopathology or illnesses of mood. Do we—in our rush to diagnose, to heal, and perhaps even to alter their genes—compromise the respect we should feel for their differentness, independence, strength of mind, and individuality?" (258–259)

Poet May Sarton (1992) reflected on the potency of her own pain when she wrote: "In the time of great tension and of splendor, I knew not whether I was joy or grief, whether swung out on madness or belief. Or some difficult truth to bend—or whether it was the relentless thrust of withheld poetry bursting my chest." Her "not knowing" sounds something beautiful here. Without a diagnosis to fight, she stays with the vagaries of her mind and seems to believe, in some sense, in the power of its difficulties.

Leslie, who is a dancer, has been influenced by the theory that great artists are prone to mental illness, and believes that she, by virtue of the work that she does, is vulnerable to depression. Her experience of depression, however, does not align with her dream of it. "I felt like I had this idea of depression from an Eastern viewpoint as a spiritually important part of life. And from the perspective of an artist, I also had romantic ideas of depression. To me it was something that anyone who is attempting to be an artist goes through, and though it's difficult it's also ultimately in the service of one's art. I was not prepared for how crazy I felt in my depression. I wasn't prepared to not be able to go outside my door. The idea of going shopping for food for the day was like climbing Kilimanjaro and all I saw around me was darkness in the world. After my illness I would turn on the television and there would be a flood somewhere in the world and I would be devastated for days. Suddenly all the pain in my life that before would make me sad or make me cry, suddenly all of it was crashing down and it was all I was. I had lost any sense of myself and any sense of positivity and optimism. I danced during this time, but I was no good. I feel now like it's been this really long journey to get to this place of functioning again. Eventually I went back to work and saw friends but all of it was an effort. Thinking about all the artists who have suffered with this did not make me feel better. I read some Buddhist stuff during it and I think that that helped because it made me feel like what I was experiencing was not so strange. But to me it did feel strange. Not beautiful, not insightful, just crazy. It felt crazy and I was crazy.

"I will say that by going through this episode I've become a much more empathetic person. I was so open to all of the pain in the world, which, though it may be valuable spiritually, at the time felt like shit. But at least now I am aware of and have felt that pain. So, from an artist's viewpoint I never knew quite how miserable things were before. Now I know. Isn't that lovely?"

Empathy is a quality that many women say has been deepened through their experience of depression. In *Touched with Fire* Robert Lowell, teacher, poet, man of letters, and admitted manic-depressive, is quoted saying that to have had an experience of extreme mood is to have known that the "glory, violence and banality of such an experience is corrupting"(29). I submit that it is this corruption that marries those of us who have had depression to each other. Mental anguish is a profoundly intimate connection.

Jamison describes the process of an artist using the anguish this way: There is an "importance of moods in igniting thought, changing perceptions, creating chaos, forcing order upon chaos and enabling transformation" (5). Many artists, writers, and poets talk in their letters and in their art about the dark effects of anguish on their work. It seems that for many of them, some of art may be born under a mood, but the refining of those earlier ideas happens in times of health. Jamison says, "It is the interaction, tension, and transition between changing mood states, as well as the sustenance and discipline drawn from periods of health that is critically important; and it is these same tensions and transitions that ultimately give such power to the art that is born in this way" (6).

Distinguishing Between Illness and Art

Kitty, who acts and sings and directs, agrees that there is no room for her creative work when depression is around. "I feel completely cut off from that part of myself. I would love to be able to work through a depression, oh man. But there's nothing. I think it's the self-hatred. There is so much self-hatred as part of my depression that I can't act. I stop myself from acting. I actually feel kind of weird that

I've had all of this experience with depression and not only am I not creative when I'm in it, I never put that experience into my art when I'm out of it either. It's like, 'Why aren't I doing something meaningful with this?' I guess I'm just afraid it will be so boring. At least I haven't figured out a way to do it that wouldn't be boring. Anyway, I wanna do comedy. People with broken legs are not asked to climb Mt. McKinley."

Kitty may not put her depression into her creative work, but she does notice a creative "growth spurt" once she's well again. "There's always actually a huge growth spurt after. When I'm depressed it's like I dip my cup back into all the sad things in my life. When it's over, well, it's like when you have a cold and then once the cold is gone you have that burst of energy again."

There is a school of researchers who specialize in the connection between madness and creativity. But predating them was the nineteenth century essayist Charles Lamb, whom Jamison quotes as saying, "far from the position holding true, the great wit (or genius, in our modern way of speaking), has a necessary alliance with insanity, the greatest wits, on the contrary, will ever be found in the sanest writers. It is impossible for the mind to conceive a mad Shakespeare. . . . The mistake is, that men, finding in the raptures of higher poetry a condition of exaltation, to which they have no parallel in their own experience, besides the spurious resemblance of it in dreams and fevers, impute a state of dreaminess and fever to the poet. But the true poet dreams being awake. He is not possessed by his subject, but has dominion over it" (53).

Anne would agree with Lamb. She is a retired music teacher who held on to and performed her job during her depression, but certainly never felt as if the other creative aspects of her life were enriched. She wasn't drawn to playing outside of work and she didn't pour her pain into the lovely watercolors that line her modest home studio today. "I was not more creative during my depression. There was not enough energy to do any more than what needed to be done every day. After the depression subsided, the energy came back and it was much easier to be creative and insightful."

But if what Lamb says is true, then why the disproportionate numbers of artists and writers suffering from depression and manic depression? Clearly not all, or even most, artists suffer from major mood disorders, but the incidence is higher than in other fields of work. Maybe it does have something to do with the depths in which they dwell.

Sharon says, "I never feel more creative when I am depressed, although sometimes I do feel more clear-sighted than some of my optimistic friends. They often seem naïve and cloistered. I do often feel more intelligent after coming back as well. Very often I feel I have awakened to the Gods and sunlight—lots of Greek imagery."

The poet Jane Kenyon wrote (1999), she says, from her soul. But often that meant writing from a place of depression. She didn't write while in the midst of a depression, because at that time, she said, "I can't initiate anything. I can't move."

"Depression is something I've suffered from all my life," Kenyon told journalist Bill Moyers (153). "I have found that when I've read any of these poems that really dwell on depression, people come up to me afterward and hug me . . . . Last week in Louisville, Kentucky, a man in the second row, who had been looking at me intently as the poem went on . . . took his hand and put it over his heart. Then he brought his hand to his heart over and over and just looked in my face. I knew that he also suffered" (154).

In many ways we accept and appreciate mood disorders in artists because they have the permission to explore them, and give them to the public and create with them community and connection. When Moyers tells her that her poems help people to deal with depression, Kenyon says, "That is my hope, because if this is just personal, then I've been wasting my time. The unrelenting quality of depression really makes its impression on people. It's this thing that will not let you go, that comes when it wants and goes when it wants. You're like a chipmunk in the eagle's talons . . . I'm trying to explain to people who have never experienced this kind of desolation what it is. It's important for people to understand that those with endogenous depression, melancholia, don't do this for the fun of it" (158–159).

In the midst of Kenyon's darker work on depression, you find a poem entitled "Once There Was Light," in which she talks of the return of belief and relaxing again into life. Here she is able to covey to her readers what it feels like when depression ends. "I really had a vision of that once. It was like a waking dream. My eyes were open and I saw these rooms, this house, but in my mind's eye . . . I also saw a great ribbon of light and every human life was suspended. There was no struggle. There was only this buoyant shimmering, undulating stream of light. I took my place in this stream and after that my life changed fundamentally. I relaxed into existence in a way that I never had before" (160).

Although like Kenyon some of us may attach a meaning to the depression we experience, if we do not identify ourselves with the arts or some other "depressing" profession, the society itself may have another idea about us. In *Willow Weep for Me*, performer and writer Meri Nana-Ama Danquah (1998) chronicles her on-again, off-again battle with depression. She includes the stories of gifted African-American women that she is close to who have also battled depression, and notices that the standard societal link between madness and genius suspiciously seems to come apart along race and gender lines.

"I have noticed that the mental illness that affects white men is often characterized, if not glamorized, as a sign of genius, a burden of cerebral superiority, artistic eccentricity—as if their depression is somehow heroic. White women who suffer from mental illness are depicted as idle, spoiled, or just plain hysterical. Black men are demonized and pathologized. Black women with psychological problems are certainly not seen as geniuses; we are generally not labeled 'hysterical' or 'eccentric' or even 'pathological.' When a black woman suffers from a mental disorder, the overwhelming opinion is that she is weak. And weakness in black women is intolerable" (20).

At Least Let It Mean Something

The late psychiatrist and concentration camp survivor Victor Frankl observed the human spirit both strengthen and come apart under the most inhumane conditions. When he was released after three years in Auschwitz and Dachau, Frankl began a practice again. He based his entire approach to therapeutic treatment on the premise that people who have faith that there is a meaning to their lives are able to believe that there is both a purpose for their suffering and a purpose for surviving their suffering. This faith helps them to thrive despite hardships. But those of us who live in what he calls an "existential vacuum" are more vulnerable to failing mental health and have more difficulty with hardship. We are caught in a "lack of awareness of what life is worth living for . . . haunted by the experience of [our] inner emptiness, a void within [ourselves]" (128).

One of Frankl's chief tenets is that "man's main concern is not to gain pleasure or to avoid pain but to see a meaning in his life. That is why man is even ready to suffer, on the condition, to be sure, that his suffering has meaning" (136). But unlike some of us, who may believe that it is necessary to suffer to find meaning, and hence believe in the inherent value of depression, Frankl says suffering is not necessary to meaning, rather that meaning is possible in spite of suffering. Suffering unnecessarily in a search for meaning is masochistic, and the truly meaningful thing to do at that time, is to remove the cause of suffering.

Frankl did, however, believe that a state of mental "tension" is necessary for mental health. This tension has to do with striving for a goal, fulfilling a life's passion, staying steadfast on a search for meaning, and the "gap," he says, "between what one is and what one should become." According to Frankl, "what [man] needs is not the discharge of tension at any cost but the call of a potential meaning waiting to be fulfilled by him" (127). He

believes that we each have a unique purpose, but that finding that purpose has become much more difficult in this
modern world. We are further from a combination of
instinct and tradition that could point us in the right direc-
tion, and more regularly motivated by the forces of confor-
mity. As long as forty years ago, when he was offering
these theories, 60 percent of his American students showed
a "marked degree of existential vacuum" (129). One of the
issues that these American students were coming up against
was the belief that unhappiness and personal suffering
were wrong, that following a path that might expose them
to difficulty was in itself unhealthy. And when they were
unhappy they felt guilty about this unhappiness, making
them even more unhappy!

So mental health needn't be a state of disguising the
difficult, nor a state of welcoming it at all costs. But Frankl
would encourage that when we are confronted with suffering that we cannot dislodge, the option then is to change
ourselves.

Gail is one depression sufferer who did just that. "I
made a conscious decision after trying to kill myself that
what I had been using to get by, my whole value structure,
it had to change. You know, whatever it was I had been
using to gauge happiness, unhappiness, what's good and
what's bad in the world had to change in order to accommodate the fact that it didn't match up. Having to reconstruct a value structure, I think that's a really crucial part
of it. Finding some kind of understanding. For me, understanding was the key to moving through depression.
Trying to come to some understanding of the mystery of
life, which has led me into spiritual studies. I have to go
back to how I'm asking for things, because the universe

will provide you with whatever you need, but you can't be attached to the form it comes in and that has always been difficult for me. I think broadening my perspective, looking to other religions and ways of understanding the world has helped tremendously. Because we all want basically the same thing. We want to be happy people, to be fulfilled. But anyone who is happy all the time isn't truly living, because one of the great things of life is sadness. For all life there has to be death."

Summary and Questions:
What does depression mean to you?

Kendall makes sense of her depression when she says, "I really think it's cliched, but that notion that what doesn't kill you makes you stronger applies here. I fully believe it and I think it's applicable in my own life. I like who I am fundamentally in my life now, so how can I trade all the stuff that I went through? It would just be denying who I am now and all that contributes to it. Plus, depression sensitizes you to other people. It makes you a strong ally and a friend and a big-time confidante."

❖ Can you appreciate the sense that some of these women have tried to make of the depression in their lives, and are you yourself trying to understand why a depression might be happening? What have you come up with?

❖ Is there a spiritual, creative, or philosophical explanation for depression that resonates for you? If so, try putting that explanation into your own words.

❖ What do you imagine you will think about your depression when it's over?

❖ Do you think depression has or will alter your perspective on living, meaning, and relationships? How?

❖ How is that key aspect of your depression that you are going to work on affected by these questions of meaning?

Chapter 3

Bell Jars and Biology

Somebody said something to me about resentment being not saying what you wanted and then being pissed off that you didn't get what you wanted, and I sort of feel like depression is a similar thing for women. We don't know that we have any power and we're lucky if somebody tells us that we do. And I don't think that's right. I don't want women to continue to be brought up this way.

—Mel

I remember learning the theory of learned helplessness in my Psych 101 class. The rats that gave up when the lever they were pressing didn't give them food. And I remember us making the connection back then between rats and women. That we as women get shot down so much by this culture that we learn to live more and more limited lives until we just give up. Sounds pathetic, huh?

—Sheila

Most of my female friends suffer episodic depression. Depression seems to be a condition of being female. However, my husband unwittingly displays bouts of depression through hostility and sarcasm, as does his father, and my brother becomes snappish and condescending when he's depressed.

—Grace

It took my HMO three months to grant me an audience with a psychiatrist authorized to prescribe antidepressants. I was hopeful about the drugs, and that stretch of time without chemical intervention seemed unbearable to me and also patently cruel, an observation I shared with the therapist I'd been assigned to through the mental health phone tree. After shrugging me off, she suggested I bide my time in their hospital-sponsored depression group. This wasn't such a bad idea. I'd already learned that I wanted company all the time, and weekly wallowing company, even if it was the company of strangers, sounded just right to me. Every Tuesday evening for eight weeks I faced a ring of those cushy blue institutional chairs and a baker's dozen of depressed women and men. Each person there seemed as frightened and exhausted and exquisitely tortured as I was. It was refreshing. We met in a small, bright room with a dry erase marker board that served as a backdrop for our two sparkly facilitators, both foreign-born women with soothing demeanors and exceptionally nice clothes. We would spend the first few minutes of each group smiling weakly at each other and scuttling our chairs around to face these two, turning our backs on a wall of windows that did a nice job of framing the foggy, darkening descent of San Francisco's winter evenings. Our leaders would take to the board and we'd watch rapt as they spelled out their special formula for wellness in green and blue and red ink. It took the form of diagrams and charts and messy long lists of "feeling words" and "dangerous thinking."

As the weeks wore on it became apparent to me that though people dropped and joined the group, the core of those who remained were mostly women. If there were twelve of us there, two would be men. If five showed, four of those five would be women. This gender disparity is much more noticeable to me in retrospect, since the things we said to each other and about ourselves in these hours together didn't vary by gender. It seems that depressed men and women are capable of hating themselves in equal measure, can view the world with the same sense of lonely overwhelm and be capable of the same level of weary compassion. But our little group also seemed to reflect the reality I'd been hearing about long before I recognized the first signs of depression in myself. Depression may affect both sexes, but when it is uncovered in the light of day and claimed by the sufferer, it appears to be mostly a woman's problem.

A Woman's Condition

For generations now, we've been hearing that depression is a girl thing. Famous tragic literary figures like poet and *The Bell Jar* author Sylvia Plath explored depression decades back and began to shed a brutally bright light on the very many reasons women may have to be depressed. Other female luminaries before and since have wrestled with depression both personally and professionally. They include artists like Georgia O' Keeffe; performers like Barbra Streisand, Joan Rivers, Marie Osmond, and Winona Ryder; writers like Emily Dickinson, Zelda Fitzgerald, Shirley Jackson, Jane Kenyon, Carson McCullers, May Sarton, Edna St. Vincent Millay, Anne Sexton, Mary Shelley, Sara Teasdale, Mary Wollstonecraft, and Virginia

Woolf. It's become more common for public figures in all realms to come forward with their depression. Tipper Gore, Queen Elizabeth, and Kitty Dukakis have all shared their stories. These public announcements call attention to the huge numbers of women who suffer privately.

The statistics go like this: Women are diagnosed with depression at roughly twice the rate of men; about 20 percent of all women experience an episode of clinical depression at least once in their lifetime (this is as opposed to only 8 percent of the total population). Currently one out of sixteen American women is suffering from clinical depression (Raskin 1997). The risk we women run of encountering our very own depression is higher than that of contracting breast cancer, being infertile, or having an abnormal Pap smear (21). Despite the ongoing stereotype of the depressed upper class white woman, research has concluded that women from all American ethnic minorities suffer from depression at similar rates. They are not diagnosed at the same rates as white women for reasons having to do with accessibility to and comfort with mental health care, and with the failure on the part of practitioners to properly diagnose minority women. But the idea that cultural conditioning keeps Latina and African-American and Asian women from becoming depressed seems more myth than reality. (Rates among Native American women are still being studied). And although they have a harder time being properly diagnosed, these women recover from depression at the same rates as white women. The greatest determining factors for depression remain gender (female) and socioeconomic status (low).

The arguments over why gender is such a determining factor are both old and new. There are the various and long-standing ideas about the relationship between depression and women's oppression. The old "learned helplessness" theory penned long ago by American Psychological Association president Marty Seligman, says that people who feel that they cannot exert control over important events in their life develop a sense of fatalism or helpless resignation that often leads to depression. Since women historically have held less power than men, learned helplessness theory has more often been applied to them. There is also the classic contention of second wave feminists like Betty Friedan that many women suffer from some approximation of "housewife malady"—the boredom, undervaluation, and hopelessness of what was at one time considered the potential-wasting life of a wife and/or mother. Stanford researcher Susan Nolen-Hoeksema (1990) has studied this more recently and found that among housewives who are not receiving positive affirmations from their partners, are lacking intimacy with them, or find the work they do at home unfulfilling, rates of depression are high. This, according to some, can be attributed to a self-definition that is dependent on the housewife role alone and to the idea that if an individual suffers from a "paucity of roles" in her life, then when that role is unfulfilling or problematic in some way, depression will result. Much like the single men who report even more isolation than housewives, not having both a work and home role is a risk factor for depression in anyone (98).

Interestingly, housewives are no more depressed than other groups of women. In fact, married, employed women suffer with depression at similar rates. Not surprisingly, both groups seem to suffer at higher rates than their male partners. There is speculation that both groups of women suffer because they are overloaded with work of all kinds, working outside and inside the home on average sixty-nine hours a week, while married employed men work on average fifty-six hours (99).

There was much influential feminist writing which, in the sixties, seventies, and eighties especially, continued to grow these and similar theories, theories which many feel still offer a poignant and resonant pitch for the unbalanced numbers today. As long as women are mothers and partners and daughters and friends, they will wrestle with the obligations of nurturing others, and they will face the question of the relative importance of their own individuality.

Psychologist Harriet Lerner (1989), an acclaimed expert on the psychology of women, notes that depression may in part serve as an indirect form of protest on behalf of women.

She believes that women suffer injustices and live lives of denied selfhood but often may find the prospect of changing and claiming their own sense of themselves in the face of their family's or society's needs and expectations too dangerous a proposition to actually consider. This catch, she contends, keeps women depressed. "The de-selfing process begins in the family of origin and is continued most conspicuously in women's relationships with men . . . to become clearer, to act stronger, to be more separate, assertive, and self-directed (are) all equated with a castrating, destructive act that would diminish and threaten (the) partner, who might then retaliate and leave." Lerner believes that this is an unconscious belief that a majority of women share. And, she says, "The position as the sick one or the depressed patient . . . further [lowers] self-esteem and sense of competence, making it even less likely that [a woman] would have a sense of legitimacy about voicing her complaints and taking a new and different action on her own behalf." (201–204).

The other thing that the depressed mind does is to shift a woman's focus from other-directed anger to a nonproductive focus on blaming of the self. Lerner says, "For many women, depression serves to bind anger and obscure its sources, allowing these women to deny relationship difficulties entirely and maintain a single-minded focus on the question, 'What's wrong with me?'" (203).

Carol would agree with this interpretation. "I was not aware that I was depressed at first—I sort of spiraled into it. I had not been honest with myself. I was very unhappy, angry, and disappointed, and I did not acknowledge any of those feelings. It started out with my having a panic attack. I had never had one before, never even heard about them, and I had no idea what hit me. I thought that I was losing my mind and my identity and I knew I would never be the same. I saw my GP because I thought I was dying. He did all kinds of tests for different possible diseases. When the results came back he told me that there was nothing physical causing the symptoms. He referred me to a female psychologist and I had sessions with her twice a week for about three months The doctor also prescribed antidepressants and tranquilizers. The diagnosis was anxiety and depression. When I acknowledged that I was unhappy, angry, and disappointed, it was a revelation! I didn't like my situation in life and I had to make changes to get out of the depression. My situation was that I was living with my husband and our two-year-old son in my in-laws' house. Everyone seemed to be happy and getting something good out of the situation except me! I felt terribly guilty because the situation had to change just for me. I had been taught to be unselfish, sacrificing, and passive. Making changes just for my well-being was very foreign to my nature. But in depression, my "nature" felt foreign anyway and I had a real desire to be well. So I pushed for those changes. I changed a lot—became a different, stronger person. I am really so grateful for the experience of that depression. I think it gave me a realistic outlook on life, and I grew up."

Previous to the last couple of decades, women were treated for their depression by therapists who often attempted to help them see themselves clearly and develop a stronger sense of their own needs. But there was also new speculation about the relationship between women's biology and depression. Reproductive hormones came under investigation and the term PMS crossed over from the vernacular to the realm of psychiatric diagnosis. Then there was the question of genetics. Did every depressed mother produce a depressed daughter? Of late researchers, practitioners, and sufferers themselves have been challenging these compelling biological and genetic theories and arguing new points about the whys of women's high depression numbers, among them the possibilities that all previous explanations are off, and even that the statistics lie.

In her seminal work, *Women and Madness*, the feminist psychologist Phyllis Chesler (1997) argued that the occurrence of unstable mood is actually relatively equal between the two sexes, but that societal constrictions lead men and women to express this instability in remarkably different ways. She quotes an *Abnormal Psychology* article that finds, "the symptoms of men are . . . more likely to reflect a destructive hostility toward others, as well as a pathological self-indulgence. . . . Women's symptoms, on the other hand, express a harsh, self-critical, self-depriving, and often self-destructive set of attitudes" (79). It would make a certain sense that women would be more often diagnosed as depressed than men, if we are to take into account these latter symptoms. Men, on their end, will deal more often with labels like alcoholic, rager, and sex addict, and are diagnosed with personality disorders and psychosis at higher rates than women. This is if, Chesler contends, they are diagnosed at all. "Theoretically, all men," she says, "but especially white, wealthy, and older men, can act out many disturbed drives more easily than women can. Men are generally allowed a greater range of 'acceptable' behaviors than are women" (78). Think, for instance, about how female alcoholics are felt to be more deeply disturbed than their male counterparts. Or how anger and physical abuse are more readily associated with fathers, and when mothers express themselves this way, communities are aghast.

We've become quite comfortable with this duality. And for all of us who have at one time or another examined our depression in terms of our gender, it makes a kind of comfortable sense. A study of hospitalized patients undertaken by Dr. Alfred Friedman found that "depressed women are even less verbally hostile and aggressive than non depressed women" (Chesler, 83). In other words, we take our female "predilection" to look inward and avoid violent or angry expression one step further when we're depressed, and turn that hostility in on ourselves. Not so far from theories of depression that Freud offered so long ago. Freidman's study further speculates, "It may be that it is [the depressive's] inability to verbalize the hostility spontaneously to the person for whom they feel it at the time when it is appropriate [that] is part of their predisposition to become depressed." There is, the study says, a "tendency to deny the 'bad' in significant others and to perceive them selectively" (83). And interestingly, Chesler has found, "it is safer for women to become 'depressed' than physically violent. Physically violent women usually lose physical battles with their male intimates; are abandoned by them as 'crazy' as well as 'unfeminine'; are frequently psychiatrically or (less frequently) criminally incarcerated. Further, physically strong and/or potentially assaultive women would gain fewer secondary rewards than 'depressed' women; their families would fear, hate, and abandon them, rather than pity, sympathize, or 'protect' them. Psychiatrists and asylums would behave similarly: hostile or potentially violent women (and men) who are oppressed and powerless are, understandably, hardly ever treated ethically or legally—or kindly—by others" (84).

Mel weighs in about this when she says, "Somebody said something to me about resentment being not saying what you wanted, and then being pissed off that you didn't get what you wanted and I sort of feel like depression is a similar thing for women. We don't know that we have any power and we're lucky if somebody tells us that we do. And I don't think that's right. I don't want women to continue to be brought up this way. Men know they have power all their lives. They may fight their own, different demons but they always feel some power and I know plenty of women who are capable of feeling no power whatsoever at any given time. That feeling just permeates everything in their lives. It's not like they can hold on to their great handball prowess when other things are going wrong—and guys can. That's a lucky thing for guys. Even if women do have the great handball prowess they won't feel it in the same ways.

"I'm sure that men go through the same inner turmoil. But they have managed to learn these other things that help them keep their self-esteem above water, even if they are going through something very deep. But as women we don't always hold on to the same little things, be they successes or whatever, in times of crisis. It seems to be all or nothing with us. We are either okay with things not going okay or not okay with it but realize there's no power to be had anyway. It may be the nature of women and I'm not sure that I feel much different, even to this day.

"Part of the reason I think I have fewer problems with depression these days is that in the past I think that a good part of my depression was not really having a sense of myself and being powerless in a house that felt insane to me. Watching my family go up and down and not having any information or skills or way of coping myself, it was as if I had to sit there and just watch it happen. I think that that helplessness and inability to come up with anything to do, other than literally just exist, was it. It wasn't until I got older and was finally free to make decisions and get tools, even if they were the wrong tools, that I began to learn to stave off depression."

If deepening a depression is a means by which some women encounter their grief while avoiding being shut out of society altogether, it is, according to some new theorists, a similar course for men. Terrence Real is a psychotherapist and codirector of the Harvard University Gender Research Project. His best-selling book *I Don't Want to Talk About It* (1997) focused on what many are beginning to perceive as a "secret legacy of male depression." Real agrees that the duality of depression according to gender holds when it is measured by how it is expressed. "In our society, women are raised to pull pain into themselves—they tend to blame themselves, feel bad. Men are socialized to externalize distress; they tend not to consider themselves defective so much as unfairly treated; they tend not to be sensitive to their part in relational difficulties and not to be as in touch with their own feelings and needs" (81). But all this outward-directedness may not, despite what we've come to believe, protect men from depression. Real says instead that what's going on is that externalizing pain is keeping men from "feeling" depressed, not necessarily from "being depressed" (82). And here lies the central thesis of his book, and of much of the discussion in this area these days, that men may escape "overt" depression, but that their true feelings are driven in their own way inward, making them susceptible to a "covert depression," and to ruined lives. Dramatic points follow: "It is clear that the stable ratio of women in therapy and men in prison has something to teach us about the ways in which each sex is taught by our culture to handle pain . . . we know that the disruptive boy is no less depressed than the overly compliant little girl. 'Acting out' behaviors are often the very symptoms we look for in making a diagnosis of depression in boys. And yet, for reasons that I have never seen explained, as a profession we have decided that when the boy hits the magic age of eighteen he is no longer depressed, he has crossed the Rubicon into the land of the personality disordered. This is not reason. This is moral judgment" (83). In fact, when men are diagnosed with depression, a blatant sort of sexism emerges. Real quotes a study involving 23,000 subjects that showed a tendency in mental health professionals to underdiagnose depression in men and overdiagnose in women.

Researchers have reported that doctors miss as much as 67 percent of men's depression because they are looking for symptoms like excessive crying, which aren't always there. They are relying on what some have called "feminized symptoms" to make a diagnosis. A related study offered psychologists case histories that were identical except for one variable: the sex of the client. Consistently, much like female alcoholics being perceived as worse off than males, depressed men were diagnosed by the study psychologists as more severely disturbed than depressed women (40). Real is asking that we do nothing short of rethink the definition of depression to include men. "It is time," he says, " to conceptualize depression in men as a wide-ranging spectrum, with many variations and differences. . . . The common denominator is violence. All of these men are violent toward themselves . . . or violent toward others. . . . And the origins of so much violence can be traced to the . . . socialization [of boys]."

Sheila feels she was taught the difference between men's and women's experience of the world in college. "I remember learning the theory of learned helplessness in my Psych 101 class. The rats that gave up when the lever they were pressing didn't give them food. And I remember us making the connection back then between rats and women. That we as women get shot down so much by this culture that we learn to live more and more limited lives until we just give up. Sounds pathetic, huh? Well, I know a lot of men who just give up too. My dad among them. I've come to believe that men and women can become equally sad, we just get sad in different ways."

Some women in this book cared little about whether the men they knew would be eligible for a diagnosis of depression. But most found it useful or at least interesting to consider. If it were really true, then would something as simple as consciousness raising or hormone replacement make their own depression go away for good? If there was something practical to be derived from this gender difference, like the discovery of a certain societal or hormonal or genetic difference that could be keeping women low, well, that was worth looking at.

Why Can't a Woman Be More Like a Man?

Stanford researcher Dr. Susan Nolen-Hoeksma's *Sex Differences in Depression* (1990) gathers and examines the results of countless studies undertaken to explain the higher rates of depression diagnosis in women. Her ultimate findings are the same as those of the many individual studies she cites: inconclusive. "The data supporting most of the commonly believed explanations for sex differences in depression prove to be meager," she says (2). These "commonly believed explanations" fall into three categories: hormonal influence, oppression, and women's personality traits. The personality traits include learned helplessness—or a depressed response to consistent victimization—and "nonassertiveness and [the] self-effacing female nature." The oppression these days means not enough avenues for personal gratification in the woman's role and various kinds of abuse. Hormonal fluctuations that effect dramatic mood changes continue to be studied heavily in women at puberty and menopause; and genetic predisposition that finds depression carried down through females in a family continues to draw some support. And then there is Nolen-Hoeksema's own theory. Through conducting her own research she has deduced that whatever the contributing biological or societal or personality factors, it is really a matter of how a woman or man responds to feelings that determines whether he or she will descend into a depression. Women, she's found, tend to mull over their problems, or "ruminate," while men oftentimes respond to problems by distracting themselves—a distinctly different response style. According to Nolen-Hoeksema, whatever the gender, this ruminating behavior is more common in self-focused people, and self-focused people are more susceptible to depression. Women may more often be self-focused and may have learned early in life that "depressed moods are unavoidable and cannot be dismissed easily when present" (172). Interestingly, she's found that as gender roles are newly negotiated there is more of a blending of traits between the sexes. The result, as much of the Western world encourages its people to become more self-focused, is that depression goes on the rise. This growth does not exist in old world cultures or in cultures like the American Amish, where focus remains without, on the community, and beyond the self. Nolen is suggesting that treatment address response styles. According to her work, "depression-prone people who are taught to distract themselves from their negative thoughts show a quicker recovery from depression than people not taught to use a distracting response" (165).

Kendall has some insights about all this. "I would argue with the idea that women are more depressed than men. I think men and women experience depression very differently; in women, it seems to get manifested through feelings; in men, through behavior. Because women show 'diagnosable' signs of depression more readily than men do, they're more often diagnosed, but I don't believe that makes women more depressed as a group. My husband and I both had bouts with serious depression. But whereas I lay on the couch and imagine who hates me and how horrible and unworthy I am, his energy goes up. He works harder, and though irritable, he's much more productive than I am during a depression. In fact, some of his best work is done when he's depressed, while my work, relationships, and life fall apart."

Gail agrees. "I think the research shows more women are suffering from depression because it is more acceptable for women to emote in our society. I personally feel that the numbers are probably equal, but because men are socialized not to emote, they may in fact not be diagnosed as depressed or even consider themselves depressed. It is okay for men to be aggressive though, so maybe their experience of depression manifests in more violent forms. But it seems to me, among the people that I have known, that just as many men as women are experiencing depression. However, I've found more men not knowing what kind of label to put on any kind of intense feeling, period. I watched my dad suffer severe bouts of depression after he retired, and it took the doctors three years to finally figure out it was depression. By then, I think the interaction of various drugs they had him on had really whacked him out. I mean think about the stereotypical concept of depression, it's someone crying all the time. Is it acceptable for men to cry openly or even publicly in our society? What are emotional or sensitive men called? Fags and sissies."

Unhappy Hormones

Whether or not men are underdiagnosed, the question of women's particular biology and its influence on depression remains valid. How much of how we feel has to do with the shifting levels of estrogen in our body? There have been some interesting studies done that track the rates of depression in adolescent girls through those years when their hormonal system is first developing. When estroidal estrogen and progesterone increase in the first stages of hormonal development, depression rises. Once hormone production stabilizes in mid-adolescence, however, those rates decline, and the higher rates of depression in girls don't really emerge until ages fourteen and fifteen anyway, often years later than these hormonal changes. There is speculation that these early-activating hormones aren't bringing about depression but that they may be creating a sensitivity in children to their environment and that girls who are experiencing hard times are unsupported by their systems at this age. Nolen says, "The number of negative life events the girls had experienced was a much better single predictor of depression scores than were estroidal levels" (49). Complicating this idea is the fact that the metabolism of psychoactive drugs in women is in fact influenced by our menstrual cycles, and, according to Nolen, some women who are prone to depression "frequently experience recurrences of these disorders during pregnancy, the postpartum period or a premenstrual phase" (71). However, she and others have also emphasized that there may also be other factors in play at this time—the stress of pregnancy and new motherhood for one. Disrupted sleep patterns and major life changes could also contribute to the return of symptoms.

Relative levels of estrogen have also come under study for their relationship to depression in women at menopause. Many menopausal and postmenopausal women who take HRT, or hormone replacement therapy, are dosing themselves with estrogen and progesterone and report improved mood. But, interestingly, there has been no correlation between menopause and a higher incidence of depression in women. In fact, many menopausal women experience improved mood with or without estrogen at this time. An often overlooked factor in this question is the hormone progesterone, which was added years ago to the original hormonal treatment for menopause: ERT, or estrogen replacement therapy. Some doctors theorized that it is not the deletion of estrogen that affects mood at various times in a woman's life but rather a reduction in progesterone. Some in fact believe that high levels of estrogen actually result in higher levels of depression.

If many of the studies of menopausal women have focused on the biology of their depressions, most have overlooked the central life changes at this time. With children leaving homes and roles becoming confused, women's outlook on life can be dramatically changed. Depending on the level of self-definition women attach to their roles as mothers, this can be an overwhelmingly positive time. When Harvard body/mind expert Dr. Joan Borysenko

(1996) interviewed midlife women, those who had experienced a depression did not stay long in that state. Borysenko sees the life changes of this age as particularly important and believes that women will undergo a period of reevaluation that soon extinguishes the depression and helps prepare them for the next phase of life.

And finally, since women suffer from Seasonal Affective Disorder in their reproductive years at nearly three or four times the rate of men, there is also speculation that hormonal secretions can sensitize the brain to the effects of light.

Serotonin Short

Equally as interesting as the question of hormones is the idea that levels of the neurotransmitter serotonin appear to be different in the brains of depressed women and men at all phases of life. Women have naturally lower levels of serotonin than men to begin with, and there is some evidence that women are less efficient synthesizers of serotonin throughout the life cycle. Dr. Gabriel Cousens (2000) found that since women produce serotonin at a slower rate, other contributing factors, such as the level of stress that a woman may be under, can lead more easily to a depression since the serotonin cannot counterbalance the stress. Men's rate of serotonin synthesis is 52 percent higher than women's (50). Serotonin level is of course believed to be crucially linked to mood. Today's popular antidepressants work to heighten levels of this all-important neurotransmitter in the brain.

Sexual and Physical Abuse

By the time they are in their early twenties, somewhere between 37 and 50 percent of American women have suffered a serious case of sexual or physical abuse. The violence of these happenings makes women vulnerable to depression immediately after the incident and often for much longer. Nolen-Hoeksema (1990) quotes an early study of battered women, which found that 80 percent of those sampled had significant depression and 53 percent could have been diagnosed with depressive disorder (91). A study of sexual abuse among psychiatric patients with depression found that 81 percent report some kind of sexual assault (95). Researchers believe that not all depressed women have been physically or sexually abused, but that this kind of abuse is an inarguable source of depression.

Crone's Disease

Though it is not strongly believed that menopause contributes to rates of depression among older women, statistics say that those over the age of sixty-five are four times more likely than the general population to suffer a depressive episode. Practitioners contend that these episodes often go undiagnosed since moodiness is often thought to be a symptom of aging. New research contradicts, saying that mental health improves with age and that some of the measures used to diagnose depression in the elderly—low energy and sleep difficulties—can be attributable to health problems and aging. Whichever is the case, a prevalence of depression symptoms among older women would not be surprising. Older women most often contend with the loss of mates and friends and family, the loss of their support systems to death or to retirement and relocation, and the loss of good health. Health problems common among older Americans are also strongly linked to depression.

Dorothy says, "It's a lot of things at this age. Life is difficult and it's going to be more difficult as an older single woman on a fixed, well not even fixed, not much of an income at all. I don't know how I do it, to tell you the truth. But you know there have always been difficult periods in my life. I don't know that I can blame it on my age. Maybe I can blame it on age as a transition period. But I think I am fortunate. I still have good friends. When you don't have much wherewithal as a woman, especially an older woman, you don't seek or find much. But on the other hand a lot of us are resourceful people, growing up during the Depression. For me depression is just my nature, my personality."

Summary Questions:
How does your gender influence your depression?

❖ After hearing from the women and the researchers, what about being a woman do you feel contributes to your depression?

❖ Have you found that large numbers of women in your own life understand real depression?

❖ Do you feel as if treating your depression should involve taking your gender into account? How?

❖ If you have a family or a relationship that you feel would suffer from expressions of your unhappiness, what ways do you see that you might be able to deal with that unhappiness?

❖ Does that aspect of your depression that you're willing to work on have anything to do with your gender? What?

Chapter 4

Family and Friends

I've had people literally take a step back from me or excuse themselves if I'm relating a story that has to do with my depression.

—Leslie

This one guy said to me, "I relate to you because I can tell that you're damaged goods." It took me ten years in therapy to stop having that opinion of myself. For someone to see that in me was crushing because I had that opinion of myself my whole life. I always thought that because of my depression, upstanding people wouldn't accept me. It's not proper to have suffered in the way that I have. I'd certainly never marry into a good family. I may have been judging myself, but the world judges that way. That's the normal world and that's why we always feel crazy in it.

—Rita

The depression was the only way to get attention in my family because the attention was so focused on my mother, who was this eternally depressed, narcissistic child, essentially. If you got sick or you got depressed, you got attention in my family. I need "a children of depressed mothers" group.

—Kitty

There are times in this life when people will accept deep depression from you. They'll accept it when someone you love dies, or when you've become seriously ill or are facing some calamitous loss. And though after the tragedy they'll shake their heads and hold your hand and maybe even fix you a meal, ultimately most will want you to run through your grief quickly. They'll try to direct your attention away from what is sad, and pressure you to rejoin them in a condition of normalcy and return the energy they've invested in you as you healed. To not heal quickly always makes you suspect. It turns you into the guy with the insistent tremor who always talks about the war, the woman who never gets over the first cheating husband. It exposes you to a light too harsh for most to examine themselves in and makes you a reflection of the unpleasantness swirling around us all.

Gail says, "I think there are so many people out there who have no concept of depression. Some of my closest friends respond in a very rational way. Like, this is an external situation, what can we do to fix it? And that isn't so bad because lots of times it's not a bad thing to look at the circumstance and see what you can do about that circumstance. But that's only half the fix. So I have a lot of people who come at it from a very calm place, especially as soon as I get emotional. I don't think that these people have any real true understanding of the feeling. I had a friend suggest I just distract myself by going out a lot until I don't feel it anymore. That might work for her in her life but I know me and I know that part of my process is to sit with what I'm feeling. Time and experience have taught me that it too will pass. With people who have experienced depression, the response you get is empathy: true compassion. Empathy is being able to feel what the other person is feeling, while sympathy is just condolences and can be pretty patronizing. I would say that the two typical responses, particularly from people who have never dealt with depression, are judgment or 'Let's fix it.'"

The Stigma Standard

When you suffer depression in the company of family and friends, everybody learns a little something. You learn whether or not those people closest to you have been as down as you are. Those who have will become your favorite people, shining examples of the possibility of recovery and the intimates who, miracle of miracles, understand the insanity you were sure was never experienced by anyone but you. But when loved ones don't get what you're going through, you all learn a lot about the misunderstanding that continues to plague depressives. You learn that others get exasperated with you, that they don't always believe that you are ill, but rather start to think of you as highly selfish and indulgent. Without a deep understanding of what's at hand, both the sufferer and their family and friends are left to toss around the easily arising stigmas that we all eventually fall victim to. Kendall's found a way to deal with all of this. "At a certain point in your life you eliminate people who make you feel bad about yourself when you are feeling depressed," she says. "You leave them alone. You can't deal with them at all. And people who respond well become your favorite people in the world. You want them close to you in those moments.

There are certain people who I can tell almost everything to and then other people to whom I just never ever say a single word. It's because I know that they won't give me the right response and I'll feel totally ripped off and lame and like a loser. I might even get irritated with the world, that what I give out doesn't come back to me. That might be martyrish, which is kind of bullshit, but when you're really depressed you don't care."

Kitty makes a similar point. In her experience, only certain people can handle her at her worst. And even then, she's often mortified at what they're seeing. "When I'm depressed, I withdraw from nearly everyone in my life. I always have to rebuild my social life after I have a depression. There are good friends but, well, I've alienated some of those people and sometimes when I get out of my depression I don't want to talk to them. But yeah, there's a core group of people and I'm careful about who I call and how often I call. I try to spread it around so I don't overburden one friend. 'Cause I just babble. I've said some things that I felt later like what was I thinking, you know? A lot of shame. A lot of fear that they're not going to want to be my friend, because my god I just exposed this horrible part of myself."

Whatever success we women have at containing our expressions of depression among loved ones, we're still regularly affected by stigma. That stigma is in a strange kind of place these days as various camps claim depression as their own. If it's an organic disease, then perhaps the sufferer can't be faulted, but those without the faulty chemistry can securely distance themselves. If it's a genetic problem, then woe the child born into that family. If it's all about environment, well, there are plenty of people raised in difficult circumstances who are doing fine: the sufferer in this case must be defective. And if it's a result purely of situation, of a life in need of changing, then obviously the sufferer is directly responsible for her suffering.

Kitty has heard all of the theories and been forced to confront them as others, even members of her own family, applied them to her. "Yeah, well, it was sort of the dominant feature of our family landscape, 'Mom's depressed.' I have a lot of resistance to medication and to being labeled because from a very early age they were watching me, thinking, 'Do you have it?' Even saying to me, 'Oh, you just have what your Mom has.' I was misdiagnosed because of that. She's been diagnosed as bipolar, which I don't think she is. And it wasn't just friends or acquaintances. I was often misdiagnosed as manic by my family. 'You're acting kind of manic-y,' they'd say. 'You seem a little happy.' Like if I was happy, it must mean I was manic.

"I also believe her depression contributed to the ongoing issues I have about where I am from and where I belong. I was raised as an agnostic Jew with no Hebrew school and no temple and nothing, no neighbors and no community. Just an isolated suburban existence with a depressed mother and a distant intellectual father. He is warm and sweet but always with his head in his hand and it's hard."

Choosing Depression

The stigma Kitty and her family experienced has been complicated in recent years. In the early nineties, as Prozac came into popular view and the numbers of people admitting to full-fledged depressions swelled, a new kind of stigma emerged. That stigma stemmed from the idea of available cures. A stigma that said, if depression is treatable, then in today's world people should no longer be bothering each other with their low moods. We all knew that there were therapists and groups and spiritual healers of every description out there, and now, now you don't even have to bother with them and the discomfort of their talking cures—now there are good drugs that will fix you right up. Whatever the reason for our feelings, we live in an era that assumes they're easily gotten over. We all know that depression is treatable. "Hurry up," we can almost hear others saying, "and get treated."

Along with this new set of circumstances comes the feeling depressives get that if they're down, perhaps they truly want to be. That is the double danger of stigma. The view that others can adopt to further separate themselves from you becomes the message that you internalize. In the case of depression, as in the case of a serious physical illness, internalizing a moralistic, punitive stance can be deadly.

In her book *Illness as Metaphor*, Susan Sontag (1993) attempted to dispel the idea that serious illness is at its base metaphorical: a sign of weakness, of failure, a giving in of sorts, a reflection of bad character. She concentrates on cancer and tuberculosis, the former disease still a mystery, the latter a mystery that before it was solved invited metaphorical thinking and blame. The stigma surrounding depression is not unlike that of diseases like cancer without certain causal roots, diseases that defy explanation. Says Sontag, "And it is diseases thought to be multi-determined (that is, mysterious), that have the widest possibilities as metaphors for what is felt to be socially or morally wrong"(61).

Anyone who has been seriously ill, whether physically or psychologically, eventually learns how different the landscape of illness is, and how many people around them unfamiliar with its hardships become overwhelmed and turn back. "Disease," says Sontag, "arouses thoroughly old-fashioned kinds of dread. Any disease that is treated as a mystery and acutely enough feared will be felt to be morally, if not literally, contagious. . . . Contact with someone afflicted with a disease regarded as a mysterious malevolency inevitably feels like a trespass; worse, like the violation of a taboo" (6).

"You can see in people's eyes," says Leslie, "the way that they feel about depression. For people who have never been there, there's a real kind of fear, as if they're dealing with someone who is going to hurt them somehow. I've had people literally take a step back from me or excuse themselves if I'm relating a story that has to do with my depression. Or there is just outright pity. Of course some people are great, especially those who have been there. But loads of people don't want to be associated with someone they think has fallen apart. Why deal with the weak? It's un-American."

Kendall agrees with this assessment, but also wonders if we sometimes can't see the understanding and even the help that is being offered us. "When people are depressed, they don't have boundaries and don't understand how to negotiate boundaries. Friends of mine have felt that no one would come to their rescue when they were depressed, but I wonder if they could even feel it when people were reaching out to them. That's the thing. You are so disconnected you don't know what's really going on. You just can't. So often what happens is this edgy thing where you vomit up all your intimate stuff one night and then you instantly recoil and can't look that person in the eye. You get depressed, you get way too sensitive."

Gail herself sees two sides to the stigma. "It was definitely a freaky thing, getting a diagnosis. Because of the stigma of the mentally handicapped. But actually the diagnosis helped me a lot. When I started doing research on it, it really answered a lot of questions for me. And helped me to separate the wheat from the chaff. Things like what somebody is responding to in their actual life versus what they're responding to in me. Just learning earlier on in relationships how to let people know how I need to be treated, I'm actually changing my relationships.

"Since the time I was hospitalized, I find myself playing the role of confessor to other depressed people. It's not like I feel like I've been ordained, but there is something about having lived through the experience and been transformed that puts you in a role for other people. It's almost the responsibility of the experience. I don't mean to weigh it down with a real heavy connotation but I feel like now it's easy for me to look and know where people are. There's no voodoo about it. It's an experiential thing."

In Kathy Cronkite's book (1994), writer William Styron reflects on the duality of good and bad responses to depression. "The single most aggravating thing that any member of the family could do would be to be anything but as sympathetic as you would be if your family member was suffering from cancer. The primary mistake would be to display lack of sympathy, to have the attitude of 'Come on. You can pull out of this.'

"Art Buchwald called me almost every day, just to say "How are you doing?" Because he had been through this just a few months before. His support was very, very valuable. . . . It was a kind of insistence, of leaning on you and saying, 'Look, this is going to be okay. You're going to recover. Everybody recovers.' In my case, the constant insistence that I was going to get well was so much more important than the medical intervention, even when I didn't believe it. There's a little residue of hope that hangs on. If I had depression again, the thing that would probably help me survive as much as anything would be my own recognition that I had been through this once, and I'm almost certain to get out of it again" (215).

Terry relates, "It's like when a baby is crying and you can distract them with something and it's fine. But sometimes a baby is crying for a reason. Maybe the baby needs to sound off and instead of sticking a toy in front of the baby you should let it cry. I think what I've been having a problem with is wanting to discuss how I feel and have somebody just listen and not judge and not try to fix it."

Seeing the Family Signs

For those of us who were raised by depressive parents or saw the illness weigh some other branch of our family tree, the idea of affixing the label to ourselves can initially be even more defeating and repellent than for those who have nothing on record. Kitty was raised by a depressive mother whom she feels was wrongly treated by the medical industry. "The irony is that I don't think my mom is bipolar. I think she's unipolar. My grandmother had a lot of depression and it's the chicken-and-egg thing. If you believe, as I do, that environment changes brain chemistry; if you grow up with a depressed, distant mother who's not mothering you because she's depressed for six months out of the twelve, then you're not liable to feel that happy about your life. Another kid might have run off and found a peer group and survived better than I did. But then if you factor in DNA, well, it's in my family. But is it in my family because they had fucked-up lives in Eastern Europe and had stones thrown at their door? Then you hear about these people who live through terrible things and aren't depressed, so I don't know. My brother doesn't have it. He has hypochondria and is obsessive but he doesn't get depressed. Girls do what mom does and since my dad is not depressed—my dad is one of the happiest people I know—I think my brother picked up on that and thought 'Hey, why not have a pretty good attitude?'

"Also, the depression was the only way to get attention in my family because the attention was so focused on my mother, who was this eternally depressed, narcissistic child, essentially. If you got sick or you got depressed, you got attention in my family.

"What I need is a 'children of depressed mothers' group."

Kendall's depressions are especially hard to deal with because they often conjure unpleasant memories of dealing with her depressed mom. "She always wrecked every special moment with a story that was really sad. Just always shat all over everything. And because of this, when things are hard for me, talking about it doesn't seem like an option. I get bored hearing myself talk about my problems no matter what kind of crisis I'm in. I get sick of myself just as I think someone else might get sick of me and think, 'Just shut up, you! Shut up!' I think my therapist is bored with me. I'm sure she is."

Terry watched some members of her family become enlightened through her experience with depression. "My dad's response to people that were depressed was that they should be thinking and acting like today was their last day on earth. That would snap them out of it. He was very matter-of-fact about it and thought depressed people were just lazy and self-indulgent. Then when I was depressed he started to understand and became depressed himself. There was always depression and mental illness in my family. It supposedly skipped a generation and landed on me. I always liked that—skipped a generation. You fuckin' psychos, it didn't skip a generation! It seems to be that there is some kind of genetic predisposition and then your environment influences whether or not these things come out. When I was growing up I learned the whole click, shut off trick. And then I became an adult and can't just click, click anymore."

For Cherise, recent realizations about her mother's depressions have given her new insight into her distaste for random depressive behaviors. "As a child of that age you don't get it, you just get that your mom is emotionally vacant or depressed or in a rage. Those are her three choices. It's not like I could rationalize it when I didn't know that she was suicidal every day and that she was totally depressed. She just told me that last year.

"There are certain things my mom always did that freaked me out. I cannot take naps. I get scared when I feel myself doing things like my mom did. I was sitting eating lunch, picking at my food like my mom, and I couldn't do it. I had to get up and leave the table."

Kendall has a similar response to some of the behaviors her father exhibits. "I think that no matter what, you draw on your family's coping styles—whether it's to use what's worked or stay away from what hasn't. And that even makes its way into your depression style. My father is always napping. If I see him once a year for two hours it's like 'Honey, great to see you,' then snore. To me whatever I can do to get the hell away from what my parents did to me would be the right thing to do. No napping."

Mel is certain of the untreated depressive connection in her family and finds their own insistence on her depression ironic. "I think both my parents were depressive, I would bet money. And I'm sure that my mother had anxiety and I would bet that my father did too have at least some anxiety. There were years growing up that my mom barely breathed, so that has to be it."

Judy felt the sting of judgment from a mother who may herself have been raised by a depressive. "My mother was completely baffled by it and told me I must not be 'living right' or I couldn't be feeling that way. Her suggestion was to 'Just get over it, you have a family to take care of.' As far as I knew no one in my family was treated for depression and there is no spoken history of depression in my family. But I only have to read between the lines. There was the grandmother who had an 'emotional breakdown' and the truth of it is that my mother herself is somewhat depressive."

For Emma and Gail, there's been no need to speculate about their parents' depression. They were told outright. Now both suspect a genetic thread. Emma says, "I wouldn't have believed so much in genetics except for depression in my own family. My mom is one of those people who is always doing things, always on the go, so I never would've thought of her as depressed. But she just came out to me this year as depressed, and it totally took me by surprise and made me really sad that she's been struggling so much. She told me over the phone. She's started going to therapy for the first time in her life. She's sixty-five."

Gail's dad "ended up in the hospital right after he retired to be treated for depression. I was twelve years old at the time and watched him completely disintegrate. So I think that I might have something of a genetic predisposition."

The Telling

Once you begin to share your own experience of depression, you are taking the first step to better understanding what happened either in your family or in other areas of your life that contributed to your depression. Telling can be scary and some reactions painful, but all of the women found it ultimately helpful.

Jean found depression all around her, but sharing her own has had mixed results. "My mother had depression similar to what I had when I was young. A questioning depression. But she was never suicidal. My best friend was self-destructive and depressive. But that was when we were very into angst about life in general and feeling spiritually unfulfilled. I may have known that they would understand me but rarely do others say anything helpful. What is helpful is that they care enough to let me be myself and not say too much that is too critical. I want them to tell me the truth but not put me down for it. My sister has started doing things with me. One day she made what I call my 'suicide watch' curtains. She brought over her sewing machine and thought she was going to lend me the machine and teach me what to do and leave. At a certain point she realized that I was in a dangerously low state and might do something rash. So she just stayed and talked and sewed. Knowing that she knew and that she cared enough not to leave me alone helped a lot. The curtains are beautiful and I affectionately tell everyone who I know well that they are the 'suicide watch' curtains and that my sister stayed and made them with me.

"I have a friend who has had a serious history of mental problems since she was a girl. We talk more openly than I can to anyone else because we cannot shock each other. Over the last few years I have had several friends in the spiritual teaching I follow come to me at just the right moment and unknowingly save my life. Still, my experience is that few people want to hear about your real lows. Sometimes they will help you through it but you can't tell them too much. I've found that even spiritual advisors weary of your trials and tribulations. Heck, even I get tired of hearing how I feel. Why would others want to know?

"Ultimately, for my family and real close friends, my depression has been scary. It has soured some relationships, though fewer than I would have thought. Aside from the suicidal thing—which people find very, very hard—I am often touchy and reclusive so I am not the first one invited to the party. In fact, once I went to a party and found I was unable to join the people at all. I hid out in another room until the people I had come with were ready to leave. Depression really is living in a different world from most people."

Cherise recognizes that pain and reclusivity. "I remember at this party, talking with a friend across the table and everyone else was cheers, clink, clink, with their glasses and I remember thinking how she looked traumatized. She and I should have just gone off in a corner because she was talking in sort of a desperate way. Desperate and freaked out. You go through a kind of pain and everyone around you begins to look like lee, lee, la, la, and you sit across the table from someone who's in pain like you and you just know."

Judy's telling was hard because of the sense of responsibility that she felt as a wife and mother. "When I was depressed, I had little kids who needed to be nurtured, and I had nothing left in my own stores to give them. It was very scary for my husband. I have actually shared the experience with very few people as there is a sense of shame still. A sense that I 'lost it.' Many people have been through similar experiences and can relate, but it took me a long time to talk about it at all."

Anne found to her surprise that her children were actually quite responsive to her needs when she was depressed. They were in their mid-teens. "When I had the real lows, I had only my children and my best friend to talk with besides the doctor and counselor. The children's reaction was sympathy and compassion and trying to please. My children were really very tolerant and loving and understanding to the best of their ability. They never stopped loving me and were very patient with my situation. Now I talk with my daughter or husband or best friend. I express how I might be feeling and usually get some positive feedback."

A New Understanding

Once you do start to share and ask for help with your depression from family and friends, you are often treated to confessions from others that help you feel much less alone. Leslie says, "One of the reasons I think it's really good to talk about depression is because of my own experience. The first person I told who wasn't really close to me had had experience with depression too. And I was thinking really, *you*? And I couldn't help it, I was relieved. Never before in my life would I say to somebody how desperate I am but I just couldn't stop myself then. Before that talk there was always this fear. I think the fear was that all of this stuff that you were always afraid of being and feeling, you are. You are that hurt and powerless and scared thing you've been afraid of being your whole life. And putting that out there, it's like all these other people are just going to be afraid of you and reject you once you become it. And then they don't. They sit there with you and they nod their head and they share their experience and at least I couldn't believe it. It's like a miracle."

Rita thinks that the support can be lifesaving, but sometimes the recognition, especially when you're not looking for it, can also be painful. "It's the same as the time I had an abortion. You can always be afraid of getting into trouble, 'cause you're not supposed to have any feelings of your own, you're not supposed to have PMS or cry or be sad or angry. And when I was going to have my abortion I just decided, 'I'm going to fucking tell everyone.' And guess what? Everyone told me, 'Wow, I went through that too.' Even men will share it. You realize then that everyone is attached to someone who has had an abortion.

"I'm always attracted to these men who have had really traumatic life experiences. This one guy said to me, 'I relate to you because I can tell that you're damaged goods.' It took me ten years in therapy to stop having that opinion of myself. For someone to see that in me was crushing because I had that opinion of myself my whole life. I always thought that because of my depression, upstanding people wouldn't accept me. It's not proper to have suffered in the way that I have. I'd certainly never marry into a good family. I may have been judging myself, but the world judges that way. That's the normal world and that's why we always feel crazy in it."

For Mel, telling and its resultant stigma can be a problem, but she's found her own way to cope. "It does get in my way. For instance, the only people I've ever talked to about anxiety attacks were people who had them. It was through a series of code words that we discovered that we both did and so from then on we were willing to have these massive conversations."

Summary Questions:

What part can family and friends play in your depression and your wellness?

❖ How do you feel about the stigmas attached to depression?

❖ How do you feel about other depressed people and how would you respond to their requests for understanding?

❖ What do you want from your loved ones and friends when you are depressed?

❖ What can you do to help your loved ones understand what you're going through?

❖ What can you tell the people in your life about how you prefer to be treated when depressed?

❖ Have you talked to your family and friends about the aspect of your depression you want most to work on? If not, how could you initiate that discussion?

Chapter 5

Pink Is for Girls

The drugs have made a big difference. I would not be taking some of the things that are going on in my life the way that I am.

—Dorothy

I haven't taken my medication because I couldn't get through to the pharmacy and I know I could have dealt with it another way but I haven't and look at me. I'm falling the fuck apart and it's terrifying. . . . I know that things are particularly tough right now but I'm really afraid that this is what happens when I don't take my meds.

—Kendall

I took Effexor for three or four months and nothing was changing for me. Then I went home and ate my mom's food and somehow got better.

—Emma

My paternal grandmother was a devout Catholic and always the picture of health. She managed to steer clear of doctor's offices up until around the time of her death at age eighty-seven. This is despite a daily dose of fried ham and cheese sandwiches, Little Debbie snack cakes, neopolitan ice cream, and "Coke-not-Pepsi" with every meal. She often joked that the Catholicism was a charade she was propagating on the rest of us and that her imperviousness to illness was a result of her being a closeted Christian Scientist. My parents inherited her "heal thyself" ethic and my sister and I can count, on one of our hands, the number of times we were examined by doctors while growing up. I'd learn later that my four-person family rarely had health insurance. My parents thought it was a shoddy investment. Instead we fought fevers and infections with Bayer aspirin and a lot of reassurance from my Dad, who, as a former first mate in the merchant marines, had spent years lancing the boils of crewmembers. This earned him the status of in-house medical expert and kept the lot of us nearly untouched by Western medicine.

As I got older, I grew my parent's aversion to conventional medicine, fighting my adult flus with garlic, stomach upsets with ginger tea, and my yearly case of poison oak with a combination of cursing and calendula creams. With my history, I was not the greatest candidate for psychopharmacological intervention. But then there had never been such an emergency in my history. After a full two months of insomnia and no abatement of my feelings of hopelessness and dread, I asked a couple of friends who I knew had taken the Prozac plunge whether I should consider the blasphemy of pill taking. Both, without hesitation, told me to do it. I was startled by their assurance. One of these women was a marathon runner, the other a bit of a witch, with an encyclopedic knowledge of herbs, who, before I'd learned about her Prozac days, I would have thought could hocus-pocus herself out of any mood. I told them I was afraid that if I took an antidepressant it was surely a sign that I was irredeemably sick or, worse, that once I started popping pills I would develop a kind of addict's weakness, and never again be able to face life's hardships on my own. They listened and nodded and admitted to the same initial fears and assured me that those fears hadn't been realized.

"There are times in your life when you need to take care of yourself in this way," the marathoner told me. "Think of it like getting stitches or other things you'd go to the emergency room for. You don't think those people in the emergency room with their blood and their broken bones are weak, do you?" She went on to advise that there was a biochemical event happening to me. "You should treat it," she said. "And so what if you find that you need to stay on the drug or that maybe later you'll want to go back on it again? If it saves you, if it makes you able to function, there is nothing weak about taking it. The weak part is being too afraid of what it says about you to do it."

These conversations helped me to coat over my fears long enough to get set up for a prescription of Paxil, which I would take in varying dosages—along with the anti-anxiety drug Ativan—for six months. I was in therapy while I was taking these two drugs, and heard again and again that this was a good combination. Within a couple of weeks of my Paxil and Ativan start date, my insomnia was less severe, my suicidal thoughts were fading, and the consistency of the air in my lungs had gone from a suffocating liquidity to a cleaner, lighter, more satisfying nothingness. I was maintained on a fairly low dose of 10 to 15 milligrams of Paxil, never rising above 20 milligrams. At 20 milligrams, a normal to low dosage, I experienced side effects. I felt the need to pee constantly. Orgasms were harder to achieve. I put weight on. And truthfully, I was not suddenly joyful. Nor did I feel my old self again. What I did feel was capable of dealing, in small, steady ways, with my new life. It is difficult, in retrospect, to separate the strides I was making in the very regular therapy I was receiving with the changes the drugs seemed to bring about. And I have heard from various professionals that low doses (below 20 milligrams) like mine are sometimes sub-therapeutic. Still, I do feel that they helped.

When I went off the drugs, I leaned hard on my therapist and friends, bracing myself for a fall that never really came. Many psychiatrists recommend staying on antidepressants for six months to a year, citing studies that show those who wean themselves as they feel better—normally within the first few months—often experience a painful relapse of feelings. If one day I am as disabled by depression as I was when I went on the drugs, I would easily consider taking antidepressants again. But until then, I am taking measures to prolong my drug-free state, all the while fascinated by the debate that currently rages between the drug fans and foes. And interested in how some women get through all of the pain without them.

Just Say Yes

Dorothy is in her early seventies now. She started taking drugs for her depression two years ago. It is a decision she never thought she'd make. "I'm a great one for carrying on, and I had this resistance to drugs. I wanted to be all natural. I had a sort of health consciousness about that. A doctor I really liked a lot wanted to put me on Prozac but I refused. The following year I went to a psychiatrist because I was just in a bag. They put me through a battery of tests because at my age they wanted to see if I was actually depressed or in some phase of Alzheimer's or dementia. I resisted that appointment like crazy. It was one of the hardest things I ever had to do. It's been a couple of years now but if you could have seen the resistance I put up, you have no idea! I don't care if friends of mine or anyone else does it. But for me it was like I had given something up to do it. I'm taking Wellbutrin and a minimum amount of a drug called Zyprexa at night. Since I've been taking these drugs I don't take life terribly big. I'm not bereft. I am having fun again. I don't have the highs or the lows. The drugs have made a big difference. I would not be taking some of the things that are going on in my life the way that I am without them. I also used to wake up about three or four in the morning but now sleep is not a problem."

The New Candy Store

The Wellbutrin Dorothy takes works on levels of neurotransmitters in her brain that are thought to be related to mood. Most of today's popular antidepressants work on neurotransmitters, but in differing ways. The most often prescribed new drugs are called SSRIs or selective serotonin reuptake inhibitors. SSRIs were approved by the FDA in the late eighties and early nineties. As the name implies, they help nerve cells hold on to the amine neurotransmitter serotonin. Prozac and Zoloft and Paxil are all SSRIs as are the newer drugs Celexa and Luvox. (Luvox is currently only prescribed for the treatment of obsessive-compulsive disorder.) Many antidepressants work in some way to maximize serotonin levels, and SSRIs are not necessarily thought to be more effective than older or newer drugs. In fact effectiveness ratings have them helping no more than 60 to 80 percent of those who take them as directed—a standard statistic with most antidepressants. But SSRIs have achieved a kind of trusted status both among those prescribing them and among the general populace because of their manageable side effects and significant publicity.

Older antidepressants called tricyclics, which include Elavil and Anafranil, make many people ill, while the even older antidepressants Nardil and Parnate, which belong to a class called MAOI or monoamine oxidase inhibitors, come with severe food restrictions. People who have taken MAOIs are well aware of the extreme side effects that can result from ingesting the many very common foods that contain the amino acid tyramine. Anyone taking an MAOI must adhere to a strict diet to avoid interactions with this amino acid, which can cause dangerously high increases in blood pressure.

MAOIs work by interfering with the enzyme monoamine oxidase, which normally clears the amine neurotransmitters serotonin, epinephrine, norepinephrine, and dopamine from the synapses. Tricyclics work by keeping nerve cells themselves from eliminating both serotonin and norepinephrine. They also interfere with the metabolism of other amines. These drugs, which include not only Elavil and Anafranil, but also Aventyl and Pamelor (notriptyline), Norpramin, Sinequan, Surmontil, Tofranil, and Vivactil, have the same effectiveness ratings as SSRIs and MAOIs. People with a history of seizures, heart disease, hyperthryroidism, glaucoma, or urinary retention are advised to use them with caution.

Drugs that are structurally unrelated to these three categories of antidepressants but also have been shown to be effective include Effexor XR, which is both a serotonin and norepinephrine reuptake inhibitor; Serzone, which acts in such a way that it causes fewer cardiovascular side effects than older antidepressants; the popular Wellbutrin, which increases levels of norepinephrine, serotonin, and dopamine; Desyrel, which for reasons that are still fuzzy is believed to alter the effects of certain neurotransmitters in the brain; Ludiomil, which works to increase levels of norepinephrine in the nervous system; and Remeron, one of a new class of antidepressants called nonadrenergic and specific serotonergic antidepressants (NaSSA).

Choosing among these drugs is not an exact science. Often a practitioner will try a patient out on an SSRI that has worked well for his or her patients in the past, and then switch to another if it seems ineffective. Some people are more or less willing to endure various side effects particular to each drug. Prozac, for instance, may exacerbate insomnia in patients for whom that is a problem. And it inhibits orgasm in a large number of users. Here's a list of the side effects that have shown up in some SSRI users:

- Sexual side effects occur in 40 to 50 percent of users, most often inability to orgasm, but also decreases in desire and arousal, vaginal dryness in women, and difficulty achieving and maintaining erection in men.

- Sleep disruptions, or "micro-awakenings," which may go unnoticed by users but can contribute to common feelings of fatigue. Also, difficulty falling asleep in some, excessive sleepiness in others.

- Nausea

- Headache

- Sweating (including night sweats)

- Diarrhea

- Drowsiness

- Tremors

- Weight loss or gain

- Dry mouth

- Anxiety

- Dizziness

- Problems urinating

There are more severe side effects for SSRIs and all of the antidepressants; these effects are less common than those listed above, but they still should be considered before you begin use. I suggest researching these, being very careful if you have an existing cardiovascular or hormonal condition, and checking to make sure none of your current medications interact in dangerous ways with these drugs. It is not recommended to take herbal or "natural" mood enhancers like St. John's Wort and SAM-e when on antidepressants.

A Means to an End

Gail and Mel both steadied themselves on drugs, and by virtue of that steadiness were able to work through some of the problems that had gotten them depressed in the first place. Gail says, "I wasn't able to really start doing behavior modification until I got on medication and got stabilized. I stayed on the [Desyrel] for three and a half years. It was so important for me to be stable for that long, to learn all of these behavior changes and know that when I came up against a circumstance in my life that was going to trigger an episode I'd be able to deal with it."

Mel says, "This is before the days of Prozac, but even on these drugs I could feel a difference. There was not so much sitting on my shoulders. I knew that the drug was giving me a lighter sense of things, but I'm so analytical that I fought it as much as anything else. I kept thinking, 'I want to figure out why this can make me feel lighter when I'm not really light.' And that was probably the beginning of a lot of searching."

You're Only Messed Up If You Take Them

Plenty of women who have suffered long and hard with depression wouldn't consider chemical intervention. Take

Rita, who got through nearly fifteen years of suffering with no antidepressants. "I don't know about you," she says, "but I felt like if I took antidepressants I was really fucked up. You know, if I ever allowed myself to take them. They wanted to hospitalize me too as a child but I said hell no, if you put me in an institution I'll go crazy." She says now she's changed her mind. The new acceptability of SSRIs has made taking them less of a condemnation of self in her eyes. "I would take them now in a second," she admits.

Of course Rita's earlier stance is one maintained by lots of women these days. When we don't know the origins of a health issue in this country, we are often willing to assign blame to the sufferer. And accepting medical intervention for depression can feel to the sufferer like failure. Susan Sontag, in her book *Illness as Metaphor* (1993), talks about how once diseases like TB and cancer had been considered diseases of personal weakness. Before the tuberculum bacteria was isolated, Sontag writes, "TB was understood, like insanity, to be a kind of one-sidedness: a failure of will or an overintensity." Valeris Davis Raskin, author of *When Words Are Not Enough* (1997), and a psychiatrist who sees antidepressants as every depressed woman's right, says, "I tell my patients that they are like the consumptive patient of the 1800s, a woman blamed for experiencing an illness that later generations would view as biological. Your granddaughters, I say, will laugh at our quaint notions that depression, obsessive-compulsive disorder and anxiety were primarily disorders of deficient character, faulty toilet-training, or moral inferiority. But I also doubt that simple biochemical models will replace simple moralistic explanatory models. Women suffer from chemical imbalances, but we also suffer from heartache, trauma, grief, and loss."

There are plenty of people like Raskin who agree that depression manifests in part as a biological disorder. But these same people often disagree on the best course for influencing that biology. For years, milder cases of depression have been treated through a combination of therapy and lifestyle changes that include modifications in diets and programs of regular exposure to light and exercise. All of these methods have been shown, in various studies, to have significant effects on the biology of depression, heightening all-important levels of serotonin, as well as other influential biochemicals. But in cases of severe depression, drugs have come to be the prescription of choice.

Chemical-Free for All

Proponents of more "natural" treatments that replicate the effects of antidepressants—such as high doses of vitamins and amino acids—argue that it is a lack of sophistication among treatment professionals who are unable to customize natural treatment programs for depressed clients that leads to a reliance on the newer class of drugs. In his book *Depression-Free for Life* (2000), holistic physician and psychiatrist Gabriel Cousens advocates a five-step program that includes identifying one's "type" of depression, along with "type" of metabolism, and adapting the biochemical manipulations of certain nutritional supplements, essential fatty acids, diet and lifestyle strategies to defeat depression. Dr. Cousens claims a success rate of 90 percent.   These proponents of more natural solutions claim that many of the side effects common to antidepressants are not found in their programs: sex drive isn't lost, there's no weight gain, energy is often boosted, and there is no mental dulling.

Sharon is reaping the benefits of these types of programs. "I have not taken any prescription drugs for my depression. I do not want to take antidepressants. It is a personal choice. My experience with others is that they change things I do not want changed in subtle ways. I have had a few episodes where I almost changed my mind. Instead I have taken supplements like 5 HTP, L-tryptophan, gingko, and St. John's Wort. I also changed my diet, and I take B12, B6, and folic acid IM. I found St. John's Wort and gingko were not very effective. But I do still take the supplements."

Natural antidepressants like the nutrient 5-hydroxytryptophan (a relative of tryptophan) and the supplement s-adenosylmethonine (SAM-e) work in much the same way as traditional antidepressants, by increasing the effects of serotonin and other neurotransmitters. The herbal supplement St. John's Wort is the antidepressant of choice in Germany and has been shown to be helpful in cases of mild to moderate depression. There has been some concern of late that users are not aware of the negative interactions the herb can have with prescription drugs, including contraceptives and medications used to treat HIV, heart disease, depression, seizures, and some cancers. The French Health Ministry recently banned all supplements containing the herb; it is now only available by prescription. Many of the women interviewed have tried St. John's Wort with mixed results. If you're thinking of taking it, be sure to research any interactions with drugs you may currently be taking and pay special attention to the dosage. The recommended full dose is 900 milligrams but that level should be reached gradually. Start with 300 milligrams and increase the dose by an extra 300 every few days until you reach 900.

When They Don't Work

Other women talk about either not experiencing significant changes or not liking the changes they did feel on their antidepressants. Emma says, "I took Effexor for three or four months and nothing was changing for me. Then I went home and ate my mom's food and somehow got better." According to Anne, "Depression must be treated with a combination of medication and counseling for it to be effective. I took Zoloft. But without the proper counseling it didn't work so well for me."

Kendall is happy with the way Zoloft has worked for her, but she had to endure trials with other drugs and their accompanying side effects before she and her doctor finally chose Zoloft. "If it means not crying for months at a time that's okay, but it doesn't mean not having an orgasm. That's why I won't take Prozac. I'm sorry, but I'm not gonna not have a sex life just because I'm depressed. And that may be the most effective drug but I won't do it."

When They Work Too Well

A number of women expressed concern that they'd become reliant on the drugs. Kendall is actively dealing with that concern. "I don't think I'll ever let myself get catatonically depressed, but for the last seven days I haven't taken my medication because I couldn't get through to the pharmacy, and I know I could have dealt with it another way but I haven't and look at me! I'm falling the fuck apart and it's terrifying. I am terrified right now that this is me when I am not on drugs, that I cry all the time and I can't cope with anything. That is scarier than anything to me. Today I was realizing that that's it. I'm not on my drugs! I want to take care of it, but the whole thing about what it means to take care of it is that you're a slave to it. I know that things are particularly tough right now, but I'm really afraid that this is what happens when I don't take meds."

Drugs Versus Therapy

In an article published by the American Association of Marriage and Family Therapists (Duncan 2000), researchers and psychotherapists took issue with the idea that the drugs are the answer to our depression problems. They claim that through an overzealous effort to market these highly profitable drugs, scientists and drug companies have unfairly led the public to believe that their emotional pain is strictly a biochemical event and that the end to this event is to be found in a pill. They cite overstatements that have become commonly held statistics, and bring to light other studies, either not funded by or not released by drug companies, which list surprisingly different results. For instance, a 1999 federal research review conducted by a branch of the Public Health Service concluded that "antidepressants were effective with only half of the people who took them and outperformed placebos by only 18 percent" (27). Another study published in the *Journal of Nervous and Mental Diseases* in the early nineties found that "Therapy alone . . . helped as many people as therapy-plus-drugs, with fewer dropping out of treatment. This review concluded with this simple summary: out of 100 patients with major depression, 29 would be expected to recover if given drugs alone, compared to 47 given therapy alone and 47 given combined treatment. On the other hand, 52 drug-only patients would be expected to drop out or have a poor response to treatment, compared to 30 therapy-only patients and 34 patients getting therapy-plus-drugs" (29). Drug companies, we should all remember, are not under any obligation to publish the results of trials that do not support the effectiveness of their products. And last year alone, Americans spent $8.58 billion (that's billion) on their antidepressants.

Many responsible practitioners will suggest a combination of drugs and therapy for the treatment of various forms of depression. And in fact, many managed care providers "routinely require all therapy clients to undergo medical evaluations as a prerequisite to reimbursement for treatment. But," says the AAMFT article, "neither outcome studies nor clients themselves offer much support for applying this two-is-better-than-one approach" (29).

Carol remains skeptical. "I only took antidepressants for a couple of months. I can't say that they did or did not make the difference. However, my mother took Paxil for many months and it really seemed to help control her depression. For me the secret is to try to take better care of me. Get lots of rest, improve on nutrition, get more physical exercise, and get in touch with friends."

"None of the drugs worked, in my opinion," says Kitty. "Except for this one that I'm on now—Celexa. I feel maybe slightly different, but it's not significant. The medicines are really confusing. Is it working? Isn't it working? My pattern has been to go off them when I feel good and then get a depression, but it's hard to tell if that has much to do with the drugs. I'll stay on this one and we'll see in the winter. Come October and November, we'll see."

Summary Questions:
Are drugs right for you?

❖ Explain why you are for or against these drugs, keeping in mind that a personal choice about taking them could remain private.

❖ Do you have any health issues that might affect your eligibility for antidepressants?

❖ Are you interested in other methods of altering your serotonin levels?

❖ If you take them, will you want to supplement this treatment with therapy or support of some kind?

❖ How is the aspect of your depression you are most interested in changing affected by these drugs?

Chapter 6

Getting
Better

When the depression lifts, it always feels like the first day of spring after a long and bitter winter. Suddenly my vision—both literally and figuratively—improves. My mind actually feels cleaner and my life more wholesome. Everything seems more possible . . . from getting out of bed to being present with my son, to setting long-range goals. I am so grateful then, for my renewed sense of efficacy in the world.

—Kendall

I wish for all of us that when we're in our depressions we would do whatever we need to to stick it out there either to ourselves or to somebody else. Because answers come from the strangest places and since we don't always talk about things very deeply, we don't get to find out from other women that these experiences are shared.

—Mel

The people from my mother's generation still have a hush-hush attitude about mental illness. They think in terms of institutionalization instead of recovery. But today's women are much freer to discuss depression, are far more informed about it, and certainly view it as a treatable illness. They aren't trapped in the same way that earlier generations were.

—Carol

Getting better is a feeling unexpected and amazing, one that takes you over with an increasing solidity until you're looking around with new eyes, unsure how after all the time spent feeling awful you can suddenly be feeling something else. The sun hits your face and you do more than squint—for the first time in what feels like forever, you feel the warmth. You hear a joke and you laugh hard enough to lose yourself in the humor; forgetting, for once, that nothing is laughable. You learn of a cruelty in the world and its meaning registers, but somehow that unbearable load of yours doesn't increase. These instances happen one at a time maybe, over the course of days or weeks or months, but they do happen. They are the tastiest treats and they curdle your stomach with hope.

For me the better moments came in stages, finally happening with enough regularity that I began to understand that I was well on my way to wellness. There was a first good night's sleep. And a week or so later, a second. There was the morning I woke up and wanted to go for a run. There was the hysterical conversation I couldn't stop having with the funny friend who wanted to join forces on a new project. And there was the day the therapist explained to me the old family dynamic that had kept me from understanding all the years of my life that there was nothing better to do with your time than become who you've always wanted to be.

How Getting Better Feels

When Grace began to feel better, first with the help of medication, later without, she described her new state as "grateful and indebted." And there is something about returning to the world after the exile of depression that seems to involve noticing your blessings. Gail's come through it more than once and says, "Now when I have anxiousness or a depressive episode, I know it's a harbinger for greater understanding. And then a series of conversations happens or a series of events takes place in my life and there is this miracle of clarity and I come out of it on the other side saying 'Whoa!' It feels as if molecular, cellular change is happening, that your brain and body are literally getting reprogrammed. What a feeling. It's almost like you get in touch with the natural rejuvenation process that's going on in your body, like your body no longer has the same depressed template to reproduce on and you get to give yourself new information."

The "miracle of clarity" that Gail describes comes for some right away and for others months after their depression lifts. Women talk about smaller things at first. An absence of pressure on the chest. A day of phone calls to loved ones that don't seem like work.

Kendall says, "When the depression lifts, it always feels like the first day of spring after a long and bitter winter. Suddenly my vision—both literally and figuratively—improves. My mind actually feels cleaner and my life more wholesome. Everything seems more possible . . . from getting out of bed to being present with my son, to setting long-range goals. I am so grateful then, for my renewed sense of efficacy in the world."

The Big Reach Out

Mel thinks that the hope of recovering from depression is sparked when you first connect with someone else who's suffered. "Once you realize that other people are absolutely going through this and absolutely feeling this way, as soon as you start hearing those voices and know that other people get stuck there, you have the opportunity to say, 'Well, maybe this isn't true, for any of us.' I had no self-esteem, wondered how anyone could love me, hire me, want to be around me. When I learned that other people felt the same way, I realized it was the 'way' we were thinking that was getting us into trouble. When these voices come up, you have to fight them, you have to have that argument with yourself. And all of a sudden you just can't stay there, and once you have the tools to know what you have to do, you can say, 'Okay, wait a minute, I don't want to be here, what is it that put me here this time?' Coming out of depression is synonymous with making decisions about who you want to be and then taking that on."

Leslie had already begun individual therapy, and was having daily discussions with herself about the pros and cons of suicide, before she reached out to a friend about whether or not to take the antidepressant Paxil. "We were on a business trip together and I was barely holding it together. I couldn't sleep at all. It had been a couple of months since I'd slept more than two or three hours a night. I'd managed to get some sleeping pills from one of those could-care-less doctors at my HMO, but even they weren't really working. Anyway, we were driving around going to meetings and I finally confessed that things were going badly. It was hard to do because even though I like and trust this woman, I also hold her in a kind of esteem. She impresses me and I couldn't stand the idea of coming across as crazy or weak with her. But you know, sometimes you're really bad off and so you just go for it. Especially when there is no one else around. Anyone spending any significant amount of time with me then was going to notice that I wasn't all there. Mostly what I did was ask her opinion about antidepressants. She launched into this whole thing about how 'the first time' she went on Zoloft, she did it because she'd been wanting to kill herself. She opened right up and started talking not only about her own experience but the experiences of all of these other women who we knew and who were or had been in similar situations. It was amazing. I really think that that conversation helped to save me. I had felt so alone before and then suddenly it was like that whole stark landscape changed and I realized how many of us were out there."

Almost all of the women in this book have at least considered getting professional help, but of those who actually did, the majority waited until things got really bad. Some are in therapy or some sort of support group or program and others are just beginning to think about it. Their actions are a reflection of the population at large—only a third of depressed people ever reach out to professionals and most wait an average of eight months to do so. Some bypassed those closest to them and went straight to the professionals when their depression settled in. Others chose a spiritual group or turned to their general practitioner. Whomever they've confided in, many have found that getting through their depressions has meant talking about their feelings, a lot. For some that means whispering late at night to their partners about how they felt that day. For others, it means drawing from that bank of supportive friends that they've given to over the years. And for still others, taking pen to paper and filling whole journals with a running record of their moods gets the feelings out.

Some depressed people will share only so much with others. They may be concerned that anyone outside their own head would think them crazy, or they may carry around some real shame about not being able to snap out of their sad state. Many have had mixed experiences sharing their pain and some are skeptical about the help that today's professionals provide. There were a few of them for whom I was the first to hear that they were taking pills. But despite what stigma may remain, nearly all of them talked freely, at least to me and often each other, about the help they were getting.

Gail started reaching out to a therapist prior to her hospitalization, but there was something about being in the hospital that cemented her commitment to that relationship. "It was one of those things, which, at the time it was happening, everything in me was resisting. It was like imprisonment. But at the same time I don't think I would be where I am today if I had not been hospitalized, because it stripped away all of my freedoms. When you're stuck in a room and you can't even have a pair of shoes on with shoelaces in them, that really sends a message. And at that point I made a conscious choice not to live in insanity. I didn't want to go back to that point again, and I believe I have the ability to not allow myself to go back. Part of it is figuring out what behaviors sent me there, learning new coping mechanisms. That's one of the things my therapist said to me early in therapy—the old coping mechanisms aren't working anymore, you have to find new ways of coping with the world and the stress and whatever else you're dealing with. If you're emotionally sensitive by nature like I am, then it's more difficult. But I think there's a point in everybody's life, even if it's on their deathbed, when the way that they've dealt with the world is just going to break. Some circumstance or episode, the death of someone, will make it happen. How many people do you read about who say they've never been depressed and then their spouse leaves them or some such thing and they have to turn around and reconstruct themselves? I think that that's part of the function of depression. It strips you bare. That was my experience of it. It stripped me completely bare. And with the help of the things I learned in therapy, I thought, 'I can take the pieces of myself and reconstruct myself.'"

Terry was skeptical about therapy. She has a light-ning fast mind, and often finds herself feeling as if no one can truly keep up with her. "When I first got out of the hospital, I was heavily medicated and I was still going through a deep depression—they hadn't yet found the right cocktail for me. I would be in these groups, these hospital-sponsored support groups, and I would look around at these people and think, 'I can't believe I'm sit-ting in this group.' It didn't do shit for me. I also wasn't ready to do any one-on-one stuff with anybody for a really long time. It just didn't seem like it was going to be help-ful. But I was in this group one day and this new leader came in who was in charge of the group. I was talking about something I had done and she stopped me and said, 'Don't you feel guilty about that? Don't you feel like you got let off the hook for that?' And I thought, 'Whoa, I could get along with this woman. She is not going to let me get away with my shit.' And now we've been meeting for about six months."

For Kitty, who watched her mother deal with mental health practitioners for years, putting faith in conventional treatment has never been easy. "I have a psychiatrist now who gives me my meds and really lets me do what I want, to the point where sometimes I feel like she's not even following my case. I don't know, psychiatrists to me are just uniformly scary people. They're either unreliable or control freaks and power mongers, or they want to use you as a guinea pig and almost always see you as a number. I see her as infrequently as I can. We do a lot of stuff over the phone."

Rita started going to therapy soon after the death of her father, but was more appreciative of the help she received in AA, as well as the straight-ahead conversations she was able to have with her mother. Her experience underlines one of the complications of reaching out: mustering the faith that others really will be able to help. "After my dad died, I knew I was no longer a child. It was very tangible. I felt beyond my peers but didn't really have adults to connect to, and people, even adults, just don't know how to handle death. I remember that they announced it over the loudspeaker in junior high and it was all so surreal. I just think that I was expecting adults to step in and take care of me, but what I realized was they're really fucked up too. It seems sometimes like no one really knows what to do. The one thing though was that I started saying to my mom, 'I can't wait to grow up so I can be with people who can handle life.' And she would then tell me her tacky secretarial work stories where all of these adults were acting cruel and crazy and I would think, 'That is worse than grade school!' It was nice to have that honesty from my mom.

"At one point, when the suicide potential got more real, I called a psychiatrist and he sent me to AA. That's where I got well. Suddenly I was with all these people who were fucked up and everyone was talking about it and there were neighbors and lawyers and mothers and friends and it was then that I realized the whole world is fucked up and nobody talks about it! Prior to that I had always been ashamed of my depression. Like I wasn't in control.

"The AA didn't make my depression go away though. The first year of sobriety was the hardest thing I've ever done in my life. You think you're depressed when you're doing drugs and crazy stuff, but then you stop and you go live with your mom and you're not going to school and you're not working and you're too old to be sitting around and you're overweight. Before I had been anorexic but then I was overweight and I was just sitting there with my depression, terrified. I didn't want to go outside. It was like I couldn't handle anything. Once I got through that period, things were easier."

Mel had started talking to professionals in high school. She credits this early intervention with setting the stage for her trust and relative ease with reaching out. "I think the fortuitiveness of being with professional people at an early age who were willing to talk to me started me realizing that there were people that were really trustworthy out there. I was able to start telling friends the kinds of things I would tell therapists too. I started establishing friendships with people who I could tell wanted to have those kinds of conversations. You kind of get a sense as to who will or won't be open to these kinds of talks. I don't have them with that many people, not because I'm afraid to but because I just know that they don't want to. But I will stick things out there and I will honestly tell you how my day was unless you're really not asking in that way. Now I'll tend not to let my feelings spiral and I'll get relief before I get the depression.

"I wish for all of us that when we're in our depressions we would do whatever we need to to stick it out there either to ourselves or to somebody else. Because answers come from the strangest places and since we don't always talk about things very deeply, we don't get to find out from other women that these experiences are shared. As I'm getting older and learning more about this, I try to have these conversations all the time, because I think that they'll keep me from getting too involved in my depression."

Getting Better These Days

It is estimated that in this country a full two-thirds of us suffering with clinical depression never receive treatment. Many of these people will eventually get better on their own. Of those women who have, some have said it took too long—that they wish they'd learned some ways from others or professionals of getting out of their depressions sooner. Working on the issue and getting treatment can mean the difference between an episode of depression beginning to lift after weeks and its taking many months or even years.

Free to Freak

I was just a kid in New England when ABC aired Geraldo Rivera's infamous piece about the conditions at Willowbrook, an asylum on Staten Island. I remember it vividly though because it was the first time I'd seen nudity on television, and they were showing an awful lot of people rocking and screaming in the buff. There were close-ups of wide-eyed patients who in retrospect were probably just scared but instead to me seemed to be the frightening embodiment of what happened when the mind went missing. Most of them were people with developmental disabilities, but we all knew that they were representative of what was happening in institutions of all kinds across the country. Willowbrook became the image of nuttiness for me, and the filthy, dungeonlike buildings, which were just an afternoon's drive from my own house, became the price I'd be paying if I ever really lost control.

Ten years later I was a psychology student in need of a summer job and my underqualifications seemed just right for the local franchise of a corporate mental health facility. This was the new generation of long-term psychiatric treatment, the kind of place that takes children with tempers and drying alcoholics and manic-depressives fresh from binges and periodically relapsing schizophrenics and mixes them all together inside pastel-trimmed walls. People were often discharged to this treatment center after attempting suicide or coming out of state lockups. But they were also coming in for much milder reasons. It was the kind of place that takes out full-page advertisements featuring skateboarding kids, inciting parents to give them a call if they're at their wits' ends with their teenagers. I became what they call a psych tech, getting paid six dollars an hour to monitor the intake of medications and corral patients for various groups. People were there until their insurance ran out. For all its enormous faults, and the rather shoddy treatment it provided, the place felt almost democratic. Patients might have been there for different reasons, even for more or less levels of crazy, but they were all there together. And none of them were naked.

We are now living in a time with legislated protections for the mentally ill. A time when talk shows and company health plans both support the ongoing struggle for emotional wellness. All of this openness is happening just in time. According to a recent nine-nation study, people born after the Second World War are three times more likely to experience depression than those born before 1945 (Lasn and Grierson 2000). And according to the head of the American Psychological Association, today's American faces a higher risk of suffering a clinical depression in her/his lifetime than at any other time in the last hundred years (74).

This is an interesting prognosis for a country that is so affluent. The current risks read much like the early statistics of industrialized England, which put the rates of depression among women at a much higher rate than were reflected in preindustrialized society. There was then and is now speculation that the more modern the modern world, the further we get from what is real and true within and around us, the more time we have for philosophical rumination, the greater the expectation that we spend time alone, and the worse we feel. "Worldwide, depression is increasing most quickly among the young and the well-off" (7). Researchers speculate that this has to do with young people becoming profoundly isolated from family and systems of support. Those countries that still have strong social networks have convincingly low rates.

Others blame today's high rates on passive participation in a life that is being prescribed for us by an ever-present media and consumer-driven society. Still others hand it to intellectual theories that have trickled down into the millennial vernacular. Postmodernism for example. "What this philosophy basically says is that we've reached an endpoint in human history, that the modernist traditions of advancement and ceaseless extension of the frontiers of innovation are now dead. Originality is dead. The avant-garde artistic tradition is dead. All religions and utopian visions are dead. And resistance to the status quo is impossible because revolution, too, is now dead. Like it or not, we humans are stuck in a permanent crisis of meaning, a dark room from which we can never escape" (80). It's Frankl's existential void. Only now it is perched squarely and frankly over a generation that has actually been taught it: a generation that must now struggle against the prevailing philosophical coolness and find something to believe in.

Better Off Than Mom

Among the women I talked to, many were struggling to find spiritual meaning for their lives that would help to counter some of the aspects of depression that they felt were just reinforced by society. However, they said, modern societal sentiments had little bearing on the mothers and other older women in their lives in whom they'd noticed depression. And they were grateful for the changes in depressing "circumstances" that seemed to make today's women's lives both somehow easier and freer. In fact, there were plenty of other circumstances that seemed to worsen depression in earlier generations, including the kind of stigma that leaves treatment or even commiseration out of reach.

Kitty thinks there is something about the limited options available to depressed women like her mother that led to treatments that may need today to be refined. "My mom had a lot fewer options and there was a lot less knowledge. She went through doctors and she went through therapists and different medications. But she swears by lithium, even though she takes so little of it right now. There is no toxicological way that this is doing anything for her. It's purely a placebo at this point, but she refuses to go off it. She was out here during my last depression and saying, 'Oh, we'll go to this hospital or that hospital and we'll find the resident expert on psychotropic drugs.' "She's been on lithium for twenty-seven years." For herself, Kitty sees a different set of circumstances. "For example, at my office I'm seen as something of a maverick, but the company is filled with people like me. In the wintertime, when [my depression] was descending, I went to my boss and said, 'I'm experiencing a winter depression,' and I felt like I could tell him that. Granted, it's a small company with no pernicious HR person but I'm just kind of matter-of-fact about it." From her mother, Kitty has learned "to not get so caught up in the depressions and remember that I'll come out of it. My mom says it will get easier as I get older."

Carol sees both differences in the professional help she and her mother received for their depressions and similarities in the lack of others' understanding. "The people from my mother's generation still have a hush-hush attitude about mental illness. They think in terms of institutionalization instead of recovery. But today's women are much freer to discuss depression, are far more informed about it, and certainly view it as a treatable illness. They aren't trapped in the same way that earlier generations were. For my mother, who was hospitalized at least five times during her eighty-six years, each depression meant she and her family had to cope with a major illness that put her life in limbo for almost a year. She suffered terribly, always attempted suicide, never really understood why it happened—but she always made a full recovery until the next time. I got professional help when I had depression and it's funny, I eventually found out that no one really understood what I went through or why I chose to make the changes that I made and get therapy. Not even my mother!

"Now, my depression was thirty-five years ago and I learned that my family reaction during that time was disappointment, lack of understanding, impatience, and worry. I find however that most friends and acquaintances react with real interest, caring, and empathy."

Sharon says, "I think that today's women talk more openly than they did in my mother's day, but I am not sure that there is as much change in the general understanding of them or their depression as we would hope. I know when I was growing up we took all the difficulties of our life as our lot and not something special."

Judy can see positive changes in women's equality having practical effects on dealing with depression today. "It's talked about more openly even though I still feel there is a stigma. But today's women have more options. For instance, when I was depressed I got a housekeeper to help with the cleaning so I didn't have all the burden on me. I think women today realize that it's not practical or necessary to be superwomen. They don't have to do it all."

Dorothy, who is in her seventies, knew that there was no room for her depression in the days of old. "I was dealing with a lot that I suppressed for years and years. My father had dementia praecox from a very early age. It was a result of his contracting syphilis while in the service. My earliest memories are of sitting on clinic benches having needles stuck in my fingers to make sure I didn't have what he had. From the time I was three I lived with a man who never talked to me, often wandered off, and inexplicably laughed from time to time. Later, I myself would have these moods and hide out. Unless I could be who people thought I was—this personality that I had developed—I wouldn't go out until I was back up again. Much of my life I have been terribly enthusiastic and upbeat and funny, but there was this other side of me where I would just hide out. I remember the day Winston Churchill died, I was living in London at the time and couldn't even go out. I was bartending in a nightclub in Soho and would just stay in the house all day when I wasn't working. I knew there was something going on.

"I was never diagnosed, it was just my way. I never thought, 'Oh my god, this is terrible.' There were harsh and difficult times, but I learned I was a survivor. I kept coming up with a new gig. If I look back over this long stretch of time, I can see that I was in a coping mode that nobody saw through."

Today, women have the kinds of options for improving their mental health that their mothers could only have dreamed. Getting better is a reality for all of us, and finding the resources we need to get better is not a difficult task. In the last chapter, the women I spoke with guide us through some of today's most successful and accessible treatment and self-care possibilities.

Summary Questions:
What does getting better feel like to you?

❖ What kinds of things can you do that will get you feeling pleased and hopeful? That seemed to help alleviate depression in the past?

❖ What simple activities can you perform on a daily basis, even when you're feeling especially bad?

❖ What does or would getting better feel like to you?

❖ What would be the point at which you would reach out for help?

❖ What kind of help would you prefer (i.e., therapeutic, medication, twelve-step programs, close friends or family)?

❖ How will your feelings change once you've dealt with the aspect of your depression that you're working on now?

Chapter 7

A Steady Future

Depression first hits with a feeling of gloom hanging over me. If I can identify the cause of the "gloom" I can get a handle on removing that feeling.

—Carol

As far as getting better from something really bad, don't look at it like it's the bottom and you ain't got nowhere to go. You're starting on the bottom and climbing your way back out, that's all it is.

—Jackie

This year I decided I wasn't going to do it. It was me saying, "I am not going to go down. I am not going to cancel my life. I'm going to keep teaching, and keep calling people, and I'm just going to plow through this, not let go of the tendrils like I usually do."

—Kitty

In her poem "The Mystery of Pain," Emily Dickinson talks about the generalizing nature of emotional pain. She writes:

> *Pain has an element of blank;*
> *It cannot recollect*
> *When it began, or if there were*
> *A day when it was not.*
>
> *It has no future but itself,*
> *Its infinite realms contain*
> *Its past, enlightened to perceive*
> *New periods of pain.*

Dickinson is able to convey here that sense of infinite suffering that so many women who are depressed experience. An inability to conceive of a start or an endpoint to the thoughts and feelings of depression keeps many of us locked in depressive mindsets, and engenders a resistance to recognizing how we contribute to and maintain this mindset.

But the truth is we can all place limitations on the way we perceive, experience, and hold on to our pain. This may seem hard to believe when you're in the midst of a depression and feeling utterly saturated by a sadness that is out of your hands. But the women in this book have all found ways to cope with their pain. And they've learned skills that will help them stay well even as they encounter more painful circumstances in their futures.

From Pessimism
to Accuracy

At the second meeting of my hospital depression group, one of the leaders stood before the blackboard and shook her head at the lot of us. Someone had just announced that she was having difficulty getting past the recurrent thought that people were monsters, that underneath the "have-a-good-day" facades no one truly cared for her and most people were incapable of selfless caring. The instructor laid her marker in the blackboard gutter, raised her hands to her hips, and said, rather severely, "I am always amazed at you people and your level of pessimism."

My first reaction was to leap from my chair and slug her. The "you people" really got me. I also had a burning desire to defend my fellow depressive. "Damn straight we're pessimistic," I'd yell. "Because we have seen the light! We are the ones who have finally gotten it right. Life is not a hopeful A, it is a miserable B. It would be to the good if the rest of you would just admit that."

In retrospect I can now see the truth in what our group leader had said. Pessimism, or what cognitive psychologists call "dangerous thinking," is the hallmark of a decent depression and we had it in spades. A defining signature of depression is the way positivity begins to ebb away and darker thoughts become the norm. When your mind starts always settling on the side of pessimism and every potential outcome becomes the wrong one, formally encouraging beliefs get nullified. Suddenly personal strengths lose their importance or seem in fact to be overblown estimations that you're finally seeing in an honest light. You and the world around you are cohorts in sadness and failure. The problem with pessimism, professionals will tell you, is that it truly is only one side of your story. To gain accuracy means to accept the good in you and in the world around you, and it means recognizing the positive potential that exists in both.

In his 1994 inaugural speech, former South African President Nelson Mandela said, "It is our light, not our darkness, that most frightens us. We ask ourselves: who am I to be brilliant, gorgeous, talented, and fabulous? Actually who are we not to be? You are a child of God. Your playing small does not serve the world." To arrive at compassion and belief in yourself often means upsetting the now entrenched ideas of personal weakness that got you depressed in the first place. It is an admission that you are good and special enough to get well and be great. If indeed we choose to end our depression, we make a leap that those who have never been quite so down may not have the pleasure to experience. But arriving at that when you are depressed can be an act of faith.

Jackie is going through a drug treatment program where she addresses her addiction and her depression. For her, the difficulties she's encountered in her life were often worsened by her drug abuse, and she has to deal today with the swirling guilt that arises from some big drug-related mistakes. "My son is blind, and even though the doctors say that it's congenital and there was nothing I could have done, I still know that I was using and that that had something to do with it. I have a lot of guilt and a lot of forgiveness that I haven't found in myself yet, but I have gotten to the point where I can accept the fact that I got pregnant with him while I was loaded. There's nothing I can do about it. It's taken a lot of traumatizing situations like that to accept who I am. I know my heart is good. My shit may be ragged, but as long as I'm trying to do something about my problems I'm okay with me.

"As far as getting better from something really bad, don't look at it like it's the bottom and you ain't got nowhere to go. You're starting on the bottom and climbing your way back out, that's all it is. You know, I have to just say hallelujah anyhow 'cause I'm not dead and whatever way you look at this I'm just gonna try to go through this. I'm not gonna take the shortcut anymore, I'm not gonna try to go around it, I'm gonna have to go through it."

It's helpful to remember that you will begin to get better before you start to feel better. Wellness is work. It requires some slogging through without rewards in the early stages, and the negative thinking is often the last thing to change. But have faith, it won't take long before the work will make sense. In this last chapter I'll talk about what some of this work involves and offer exercises that many of these women found to be particularly important in taking them not only from pessimism to accuracy but out from under the cover of blueness for good.

Think Me Well

There are various theoretical frameworks that treatment professionals use when working with depressives. Cognitive theory has been shown to be the most successful for the treatment of depression. Proponents of cognitive theory recommend correcting the negative and illogical thinking that is believed to be one of the most significant factors of depression. Depressed people often attribute bad events to themselves, to causes that are internal and unworkable or unchangeable; whereas others often attribute those same events to external causes and to causes that can change over time. The truth is there are various causes for bad events, and once again, the more pessimistic a person, the less able they are to see a variety of explanations. Cognitive theorists and therapists believe that people construct their depressions through a combination of negative thoughts and feelings and so are just as able to effectively deconstruct them. There are other types of therapy, and the feelings of support that are inherent in the therapeutic process are helpful in an overall sense, but to really reverse depressions and protect yourself from future episodes, most professionals agree that you must make critical changes in the way you look at and deal with your life. Cognitive therapy's practical and active framework is the quickest way there.

When my feelings of grief and helplessness were at their worst I remember thinking that every positive emotion, event, and thought I'd experienced in the first thirty years of my life was a direct result of mistaken perspective. I was able to deflate love to a manipulation that kept people from walking alone in the world. Accomplishments turned into hollow accolades that betrayed the stupidity of those who'd bestowed them on me; and the joy and laughter shared by those around me seemed a perversion or ignorance of debilitating truth that I should never again allow myself to engage in. I'd finally arrived at an eternal truth. Happiness was foolishness.

I've now had the experience—after consuming depression literature, attending groups, getting prolonged therapy, and talking these perspectives through with countless people—of trying a positive perspective on, just like one might try on a new coat. Learning to look at the way I attributed success outside myself and the clatter of negativity that my brain consistently produced, I began to see that if I chose to, I could play with this style of thinking and being. The techniques I used at first seemed forced and simplistic and Pollyannaish. So in the beginning I used them as a kind of experiment. I was desperate to feel better and willing to indulge this idea, even if it did seem circumspect. When I got praise from an editor at a magazine I was beginning to write for, I decided to disregard the voice in my head telling me she either knew nothing about the subject I'd just covered or gushed in an identical way to all of her contributors. Instead I dabbled in the possibility that after publishing successfully for years, I might do an okay job of writing every once in a while. This led to my pitching a larger story to her the following week and getting a yes. I found that accepting her belief in my competence helped me to approach the interviews for that story with a new level of interest and assuredness. The more I played this game, the more pleasant my days became. I liked the feel and look of this new coat. It slowly began to change me.

One Step Beyond

The women I spoke with used and praised the following techniques in conjunction with the help they reached out for, the antidepressants they took, the spiritual practice they began or renewed, and the exercise and relaxation techniques they still use. These are all cognitive-behavioral techniques, and are some of the most commonly prescribed these days. The essence of the assumption that treatment professionals are making when they suggest them is that irrational thoughts and beliefs, a tendency to overgeneralize singular negative events, a generally pessimistic outlook on life, a constant focus on problems and failures, and a negative self-assessment all promote depression. Here are some of the ways they believe we can undo the effects of these cognitive downers and their related behavioral choices. This is not a comprehensive description of cognitive-behavioral techniques (see the self-help workbooks *Thoughts & Feelings* (McKay et al. 1997) and *The Depression Workbook* (Copeland 1992) for more techniques—both are listed in the references section of this book) but it is a good place to start.

Countering Thoughts

. . . The person perceives these thoughts as though they are by reflex—without any prior reflection or reasoning; and they impress him as valid. (Beck 1976)

You think automatically. And so the thoughts you're thinking often seem to be generated from some reasonable place and to reflect your life and experience with some accuracy. You believe them; they are spontaneous, after all, and they are often persistent. You may not ever share these thoughts with others, but they do a good part in shaping your feelings about yourself. When you're depressed you often automatically think obsessive thoughts about negative past events and loss. Psychologists suggest making a running record of these automatic thoughts. When you're feeling bad, write down what the words are that are running through your head. If it's an image, describe the image. It will soon become clear that your thinking patterns, often patterns that you are not consciously aware of, limit you and contribute to keeping you depressed. Cognitive-behavioralists describe eight limited thinking patterns. The descriptions offered here are taken from the classic cognitive workbook, *Thoughts & Feelings* (McKay et al. 1997). See if you can recognize yourself in them.

1. Filtering: You focus on the negative details while ignoring all the positive aspects of a situation.

2. Polarized Thinking: Things are black or white, good or bad. You have to be perfect or you're a failure. There's no middle ground, no room for mistakes.

3. Overgeneralization: You reach a general conclusion based on a single incident or piece of evidence. You exaggerate the frequency of problems and use negative global labels.

4. Mind Reading: Without their saying so, you know what people are feeling and why they act the way they do. In particular, you have certain knowledge of how people think and feel about you.

5. Catastrophizing: You expect, even visualize disaster. You notice or hear about a problem and start asking, "What if?" What if tragedy strikes? What if it happens to you?

6. Magnifying: You exaggerate the degree or intensity of a problem. You turn up the volume on anything bad, making it loud, large, and overwhelming.

7. Personalization: You assume that everything people do or say is some kind of reaction to you. You also compare yourself to others, trying to determine who is smarter, more competent, better looking, and so on.

8. Shoulds: You have a list of ironclad rules about how you and other people should act. People who break the rules anger you, and you feel guilty when you violate the rules.

When you feel a depressed mood coming on or worsening, write it down and rate its severity. Use a scale of 1 to 5 or 1 to 100. Make note of what the situation was that elicited the mood. Next, write down your automatic thoughts and images and try to see which of the aforementioned eight patterns they fall into. Label them. List what evidence you have that supports the thought. And then begin to construct counter thoughts. What are some other objective and less negative views on the situation? If your perspective is always one of loss, write down what you do have in the situation and your life in general that remains positive. (This is not an attempt to superficially cheer you up, but rather to test the absolute truth you've assigned the negative statement.) Write down evidence that supports this counter thought. After doing this, rate your mood again. Look over what you've written and notice how clarifying what contributed to the mood and suggesting alternatives to the arising thoughts helps you gain a more realistic perspective.

Some women found this technique so worthwhile that they were inspired to begin action plans to cement their alternative thoughts. For example, Mel talks about wanting constant reminders that things in her life weren't as negative as her mind would have had her believe. "I suggest you write yourself positive counter statements in a journal," she says. "You need them available and accessible or you need to have heard them so many times that you happen to hear them right when you need them. I have written notes and stuck them all over my house. One of my notes said 'Yes!' That's just about the worst thing you can say to someone who's depressed. You don't want to be looking at a big yes with an exclamation point, because you're thinking 'No!' You're thinking 'Yes what?' Or, 'I don't feel anything so it pisses me off to see that huge "Yes!" up there.' And then all of a sudden it just kind of kicks you. It pissed me off to see that word because I could no longer be there in my hood, not able to see more than a foot and a half in front of me."

Sheila talks about checking in with people when her negative thoughts about how they see her get out of control. She finds if she does this it helps her resist a downward spiral. "It used to be that when something was feeling bad between me and someone else, I would just let it fester and feel bad about myself. Like, this person was realizing what a jerk I was and there was nothing I could do about it. I was a jerk after all! That was what my mind was always saying. I communicate with people now. I let them know when I think something might be getting to them. I ask. Sometimes they are upset with me, but it's never as bad as I think. And once we talk about it it's over and we both feel like we can still be friends."

A variation on this process is something called "thought stopping." When an unpleasant thought arises, the idea is to concentrate on that thought for a short time, then interrupt yourself and get it out of your mind. This can be accomplished by saying "Stop!" or doing something like snapping your fingers or clapping your hands. You then switch to pleasant thoughts—a lovely image or a favorite memory. This can be repeated as often as necessary until the unwanted thought recedes. This is an especially helpful exercise if you experience anxiety with your depression, as a majority of women do. When an anxiety-producing thought enters your mind, stop it right away. You'll be amazed at the control you are able to have over your mind.

Mel's reliance on the "Yes!" notes in her house says something about the regularity with which you need to practice both of these techniques. Soon it will become apparent that when you hold a positive counter statement in your mind, you begin to feel better. Enough of this countering and you'll begin to see the fallacies inherent in negative thinking. Eventually you'll be able to come up with a positive counter to a negative statement with very little prompting. When you read of someone's accomplishments and think automatically, "I have wasted my life," you will know right away that you can think instead, "I have done a lot with my life as well, and I will continue to do much that is worthwhile and important to me."

An important addendum to these ideas for changing negative thought patterns is to regularly and consciously notice and acknowledge the positive things in and around your life. This will help you balance out your negativity. Stop regularly throughout the day to see if you can find anything positive, beautiful, fascinating, or serene happening around you. Have you heard a joke that is still echoing in your head? Seen a store clerk deal gently with an older person? Felt a breeze come in your bedroom or office window that reminded you of the wonder of the natural world around you? Take some time before you go to sleep each night and reflect on the positive things that happened today. And finally, learn to extend this gentler, more positive outlook into your past. Acknowledge how many of the dreams you had as a child have been achieved: to experience a relationship, get through school, bring home a paycheck of your very own. Try not to take all that you've done for granted. It is impressive and just as important as what you may still want to accomplish. Finally, fill your space with photos and mementos of people or places that you love. This is especially worthwhile if you are having some suicidal feelings. It is important to remember the good times and pleasure that life can also afford you.

Reviving Self-Worth

The same inner voice that keeps us in the realm of negativity also undermines the feelings of self-worth we all need to participate truly in our lives. When you are depressed you often feel as if you are not a significant member of society, as if by not enthusiastically participating you are somehow lazy. You feel as if you screw up everything that you try anyway, and as if you don't even have the right to be feeling these feelings! Depression is not a sign of personal weakness—millions of very accom-

plished people have suffered from depression—nor is it a
sign that you are in some way flawed or destined to remain
down. Nearly everyone recovers from depression, even
long-term debilitating depression, and gross generalizations
about how flawed you are, as we've just learned, are
always inaccurate. Part of recovering from depression is
being compassionate with yourself and learning to trust
that what you are going through is significant and may in
fact be affected by the unrealistic and superficial ways in
which we assign people worth in this society.

Jackie has spent time in a homeless shelter as she's
gone through drug treatment. She hates being there and
her feelings of self-worth plummet every time she enters
the building. "Sometimes I'll have to laugh to keep from
crying because it's not where I want to be, but I also
remember it's not where I used to be. I'm not down so far.
Then I'm always grateful because it could be worse. I got
my Bible, I read my Bible, my little piece of scripture. It
reminds me about what's important in this life. And how
just because I'm suffering or in a bad place right now does
not mean I am a bad person. I love my son, I'm getting
better for him and me. That's something."

Work to counter thoughts and feelings that inhibit
your feelings of self-worth. Like Jackie, learn to change
your perspective on mistakes by admitting them, but then
instead of punishing yourself, both ask yourself what the
extenuating circumstances were and what you might be
able to take away from the experience. Jackie meets with a
supportive group of women nearly every day who want to
see her succeed. Try hard to surround yourself with people
who are good to you, and minimize the time you spend
with meanies. If you are being criticized, remember that

depressed people often overblow criticisms. Ask yourself if the criticism really has merit, or whether it's a question of opinion. Consider the source. On the other end, accept compliments and enjoy them.

Finally, recognize and credit yourself for your accomplishments and reward yourself regularly with things that bring you relief and some pleasure. You are worth it.

Getting Going

It can feel like a monumental effort when you're depressed to get yourself vertical. But the problem with staying inactive is that it serves to worsen your sense of yourself as a pathetic creature and deepen your depression. Many of the women found that if they did something every day, even if it was something small, they were able to get through the day with less pain. Sharon has been battling depression hard for the last five years and cannot do all that she'd like to when she's down, but still does what she can. "Sometimes I will go a month and sometimes a few weeks without feeling depressed," she says. "I would say overall in the last five years I have been depressed at least half the time. When I am depressed the house does not get cleaned. I find it very hard to think or connect with people on a social basis and I cannot do one more thing than what I am obliged to do. But I do go to work and go to school. If I am able to try anything I work in my garden or go out with my sister or friends—usually not more than one or two people. I watch television if it is really bad—it deadens a kind of dangerously compulsive suicidal thought. If I have enough energy I walk. If I can do something like clean house or water the yard, it always helps."

Eventually, the women say, this kind of regular engagement, even if it at times seems ridiculously limited, begins to help. They start working up to doing more and adding things to their day that they enjoy. This makes rolling off the pillows feel more worthwhile and helps remind them of pleasure again. Often when we're depressed we anticipate that anything we do will have a negative cast, and our normal feelings of motivation are usually absent. The reality, however, is that most depressed people report finding that once they actually do something, they enjoy it or find it more satisfying than they had anticipated. The answer for many women has been to do something despite a lack of motivation. Once you do get going, the motivation usually follows.

Leslie found that by creating a schedule for herself both of things that she had to do (pay bills, do some work, shop for food), and things that she wanted to do (walk, talk to friend[s], start new dance class), she got out from under the voices that had been keeping her flat for weeks. The voices that said, "What's the point in getting up, there's nothing for me to do, none of it matters . . ."

"I have to really force myself at first to believe that there is anything worthy of my attention and effort when I am depressed," Leslie says. "Making little lists and schedules helps me to see that even if I'm not changing the world every day, I do have the energy to do some things, and at the end of the day I can go back over the lists and feel good about my efforts. Eventually it makes more sense to get out of bed than to stay there. It also helps me see how much I do accomplish in my life on a regular basis. That's a good lesson to learn."

It's a good idea to keep your plans simple at first, so they can be accomplished and you don't feel overwhelmed. If there is something difficult that you really need or want to do, try breaking it down into doable parts. Write out the parts as steps and do what you can. Often, when the steps are in front of you, the task seems less daunting.

Exercise, Diet, and Relaxation

Grace and Brenda are both runners. Cherise goes for a bike ride every day. Dorothy gives and gets professional massages. Kendall swims and plays in the park with her young child. Anne has so mastered the art of tai chi in midlife that she's been certified to teach. Kitty has done a lot of meditation over the years. All of the women talk about the regular ways in which they've incorporated relaxation and exercise into their lives. Relaxation is essential in helping depressed people quiet their minds, sleep better, and get closer to the essential part of themselves that a depressed mind often obscures. And exercise has been prescribed for years now as an effective control against milder forms of depression. Some people find the idea of exercising daunting when they are dealing with the feelings of fatigue and the aches and pains that accompany depression. However, even very slow exercise, like gentle stretching or easy walking, has been shown to help lift depression. Researchers have also found that diet plays a significant role in our moods. Author Mary Ellen Copeland (1992) found that her subjects with mood disorders indulged, to their detriment, in foods that exacerbated their depression, such as foods that were "high in sugar (especially chocolate), beverages that contain caffeine, and salty foods" (242). Copeland and others have found that there are also certain foods that actually *raise* your serotonin levels. "A diet that is high in complex carbohydrates can increase your level of serotonin. . . . Foods that are high in complex carbohydrates include whole grain breads, pasta, grains (such as rice, millet, and quinoa), potatoes, and vegetables, especially those in the cabbage family. . . . I find—and my findings are corroborated by people in the study and people who have attended my workshop—that my [bad food] cravings decrease when I am on a high complex carbohydrate diet, and I feel better" (248). There are a number of books that deal directly with this question and go into great detail both about the mental health benefits of certain foods and the possibility that food allergies can contribute to depression. Remember if you are taking an MAOI inhibitor to be very careful about following any kind of new diet.

Mel found that once she started both taking a walk every day and cutting down on her intake of sugar, her energy level and her perspective on her day dramatically improved. "I started exercising a lot and watching my diet when my depression and anxiety were getting bad. I think the anxiety was an outgrowth of the depression and it was trying to tell me that I had to take care of my body and that I had no choice or I was going to die. I wanted to fall apart with that feeling. At the time I was wanting to be depressed and once I read the books that said exercise and diet are really important, I thought fuck that, I don't want to do that, I just want it to go away. Funny thing was once I started doing those things it did start to go away. I was willing to try because my moods felt life-threatening to me. Depression and anxiety can throw you into a spiral. Diet and exercise help you to get a hold on that spiral."

Relaxation is a wonderful coping skill to master, whether you are in the midst of a depression or sensing the kind of stress that contains the possibility of a recurrence. This is relaxation in an "active" sense, not the kind of unwinding that happens when going to a movie or napping. Once mastered, relaxation techniques can be used anywhere, anytime to keep stress levels low whatever your mood. Psychologists and therapists testify that relaxation is a fabulous tool that helps clients speed up their recovery from depression and decrease the ill effects that often precede new episodes. Deep relaxation causes a reaction in the body that's the absolute opposite of the reaction caused by the anxiety associated with depression.

Some of the women used relaxation tapes—either audio or video tapes—while others learned deep breathing and meditation methods on their own that they then incorporated into their daily life. There are two highly effective methods that can help you achieve a deeply relaxing state fairly quickly. The first, abdominal breathing, helps you get beyond the high and shallow chest breathing that keeps many of us in a state of agitation. All it involves is concentrating on your breath by resting a hand on your abdomen and breathing deeply in and out so that your hand rises and falls. Count as you do this. If thoughts intrude, just return to number one and begin counting again. The second technique is called progressive muscle relaxation and involves stretching out on your back and relaxing the muscle groups that line your body, from your toes to the top of your head. Divide your body up into your legs, midsection, arms, and head, and as you inhale and then exhale deeply, concentrate on one section of your body. Tighten the muscles as you inhale and concentrate, release as you exhale. It is suggested that you practice this exercise daily at first. This will help you to achieve a deeper state of relaxation more quickly. According to McKay et al. (1997), after some months of practice people report that "the amount of anxiety, anger, or other painful emotions that habitually come up in your life will significantly diminish" (59).

Strategies for Staying Above the Blue

Whatever has worked to loosen our depression in the past can always be repeated when depression feels as if it may begin to loom again. About half of the women in this book have had more than one bout of depression. Researchers and clinicians, as well as the women here, explain this phenomenon in various ways. Some are of the "once-touched, forever vulnerable" school, where evidence of depression early on may warrant a consideration of a biological or developmental issue that leaves one open to reoccurrence. Others subscribe to the "causal factors" school, where depression is an outgrowth of a way of life or a life change or event and so eases along with the reduction of associated stress. Still others feel that depression has a kind of unpredictable life of its own: that it may mess us up just the once, to teach us a necessary lesson, and only return again if its presence is warranted.

Jane Kenyon (1999) has said: "When you get to be my age and you've lived with depression for a number of years, you begin to have a context for believing that you will feel better at some point. You have been through it enough times so that you know, sooner or later, if you can just stick it out, it's going to lift. It's going to be better" (163). It's important once you've begun to feel better to be able to identify the early signs of depression in yourself. This will help you nip it in the bud in the future and keep you aware of how you are responding to situations and life events. Make a list of your early warning signs and try to imagine how you'll respond to these signs. Here's what some of the women have said:

Kitty: "It starts out physiologically and it just feels like a heaviness; then there is a dying out of anything positive or optimistic, but it starts out at first as just a little bit less and then a little bit less. This year I decided I wasn't going to do it. It was me saying, 'I am not going to go down. I'm not going to cancel my life. I'm going to keep teaching, and keep calling people, and I'm just going to plow through this, not let go of the tendrils like I usually do.'"

Carol: "Depression first hits with a feeling of gloom hanging over me. If I can identify the cause of the 'gloom' I can get a handle on removing that feeling. I now recognize the depressive symptoms before they hit. I become aware of the 'possibility' of these feelings becoming part of me rather than already being part of me. I usually have the threat of only one at a time to deal with, the powerlessness or the energy loss, and I make sure I don't obsess over these feelings as I go through them. I also tend to my physical self and make sure I don't get run down."

Deirdre: "Sometimes I talk to myself about the pain and sometimes I write it out in a journal. That way I make the pain into a little something and it takes it out of me for a while."

Gail, whose therapy for depression has helped her learn to accept the balance of happiness and difficulty in her life, notes, "I guess I know I've moved out of a period of melancholy when I'm focusing on the moment again. But then, melancholy is an essential ingredient of my personality. The focus isn't so much on being light and 'happy' as it is just at peace and in the moment. 'Happy' is an illusion. There will always be some circumstance, some external factor that keeps everyone from happiness. Americans think happiness is like the pot of gold at the end of the rainbow. Well I've got news for you, it ain't. It's not a payoff, it is a constant choice. And the quickest way to happiness I know is to not deny what you are feeling in any given moment, and know and simply have faith that 'this too will pass.'"

What Works Best

Depression expert John Preston, the author of *Lift Your Mood Now* (2001), believes that there are four keys to healing quickly for everyone. They are:

1. Take action to get professional help. This can mean psychotherapy or psychotherapy and medication, and/or professionally-led support groups. For some people, professional help may come in the guise of a pastor or spiritual teacher, but be

sure to explain to this person that you need help with your depression.

2. Learn as much as you can about depression and be sure that loved ones learn about it too. Their support during this time is crucial.

3. Develop an "attitude of compassion for yourself." Can the self-criticism.

4. Adopt an "action-oriented strategy that pulls out all the stops." In other words, do everything you can as often as you can to get better. Toss together all kinds of self-help approaches: talking, nutrition, improved sleep, stress relief, regular exercise, time for enjoyment, journal writing, etc., and concentrate on working yourself out of your depressive state.

This is an obviously quick list and may sound too simple to some. But the truth is that we all do get through these deep and difficult days, and in much the same way. Professionals see patterns to wellness, just as they do patterns to depression. And even though there are as many distinguishing elements to the stories about falling into and out of depression as there are people who have been there, in the end depression itself, Styron's "inexplicable" force, is by all accounts a common human experience. It need not stop, elude, or permanently disfigure us, and, as many women have found, we can grow and change into something smarter and stronger when we get the better of it.

I hope that the women who have shared their stories here have helped you to see the importance of sharing and understanding your own experience of depression, and then choosing whichever of the paths to wellness resonates best for you. They and I wish you strength as you make your way through your story, and compose a hopeful ending of your very own.

References

American Psychiatric Association. 1994. *Diagnostic and Statistical Manual of Mental Disorders, Fourth Edition.* Washington, D.C.: American Psychiatric Association.

Beck, A. T. 1976. *Cognitive Therapy and the Emotional Disorders.* New York: International Universities Press.

Borysenko, Joan. 1996. *A Woman's Book of Life: The Biology, Psychology, and Spirituality of the Feminine Life Cycle.* New York: The Berkley Publishing Group.

Chesler, Phyllis. 1997. *Women and Madness.* New York: Four Walls Eight Windows.

Cousens, Gabriel. 2000. *Depression-Free for Life: An All-Natural, 5-Step Plan to Reclaim Your Zest for Living.* New York: HarperCollins Publishers.

Copeland, Mary Ellen. 1992. *The Depression Workbook: A Guide for Living with Depression and Manic Depression.* Oakland, Calif.: New Harbinger Publications.

Cronkite, Kathy. 1994. *On the Edge of Darkness.* New York: Dell Publishing.

Danquah, Meri Nana-Ama. 1998. *Willow Weep for Me: A Black Woman's Journey Through Depression.* New York: The Ballantine Publishing Group.

Duncan, Barry, Scott Miller, and Jacqueline Sparks. 2000. Exposing the mythmakers. *Family Therapy Networker, March/April, 24–53.*

Epstein, Mark. 1999. *Going to Pieces Without Falling Apart: A Buddhist Perspective on Wholeness.* New York: Broadway Books.

Frankl, Victor E. 1984. *Man's Search for Meaning.* New York: Pocket Books.

Jack, Dana Crowley. 1991. *Silencing the Self: Women and Depression.* New York: HarperCollins Publishers.

Jamison, Kay Redfield. 1993. *Touched with Fire: Manic-Depressive Illness and the Artistic Temperament.* New York: The Free Press.

———. 1996. *An Unquiet Mind: A Memoir of Moods and Madness.* New York: Vintage.

———. 1999. *Night Falls Fast: Understanding Suicide.* New York: Alfred A. Knopf.

Kenyon, Jane. 1999. *A Hundred White Daffodils.* St Paul, Minn.: Graywolf Press.

Lasn, Kalle, and Bruce Grierson. 2000. America the blue. *Utne* June/July 75–81.

Lerner, Harriet. 1989. *Women in Therapy.* New York: Harper & Row, Publishers.

McKay, Matthew, Patrick Fanning, and Martha Davis. 1997. *Thoughts & Feelings: Taking Control of Your Moods and Your Life.* Oakland, Calif.: New Harbinger Publications.

Nolen-Hoeksema, Susan. 1990. *Sex Differences in Depression*. Stanford, Calif.: Stanford University Press.

Preston, John. 2001. *Lift Your Mood Now*. Oakland, Calif.: New Harbinger Publications.

Raskin, Valerie Davis. 1997. *When Words Are Not Enough: The Women's Prescription for Depression and Anxiety*. New York: Broadway Books.

Real, Terrence. 1997. *I Don't Want to Talk About It: Overcoming the Secret Legacy of Male Depression*. New York: Fireside.

Sarton, May. 1992. *Journal of a Solitude*. New York: W. W. Norton & Company.

Showalter, Elaine. 1985. *The Female Malady: Women, Madness, and English Culture*. 1830-1980. New York: Penguin.

Sontag, Susan. 1993. *Illness As Metaphor and AIDS and Its Metaphors*. New York: Anchor Books.

Styron, William. 1990. *Darkness Visible: A Memoir of Madness*. New York: Vintage Books.

Thompson, Tracy. 1996. *The Beast: A Journey Through Depression*. New York: Plume

© Julie Feinstein

Lauren Dockett writes about women, political issues, and the arts for various publications. The coauthor of *Facing 30: Women Talk About Constructing a Real Life and Other Scary Rites of Passage*, she lives in Oakland, California.

Some Other New Harbinger Titles

Pregnancy Stories, Item PS $14.95

The Women's Guide to Total Self-Esteem, Item WGTS $13.95

Thinking Pregnant, Item TKPG $13.95

The Conscious Bride, Item CB $12.95

Juicy Tomatoes, Item JTOM $13.95

Facing 30, Item F30 $12.95

The Money Mystique, Item MYST $13.95

High on Stress, Item HOS $13.95

Perimenopause, 2nd edition, Item PER2 $16.95

The Infertility Survival Guide, Item ISG $16.95

After the Breakup, ATB $13.95

Claiming Your Creative Self, Item CYCS $15.95

The Self-Nourishment Companion, Item SNC $10.95

Serenity to Go, Item STG $12.95

Spiritual Housecleaning, Item SH $12.95

Goodbye Good Girl, Item GGG $12.95

Under Her Wing, Item WING $13.95

Goodbye Mother, Hello Woman, Item GOOD $14.95

Consuming Passions, Item PASS $11.95

Binge No More, Item BNM $14.95

The Mother's Survival Guide to Recovery, Item MOM $12.95

Women's Sexualities, Item WOSE $15.95

Undefended Love, Item UNLO $13.95

Call **toll free, 1-800-748-6273,** or log on to our online bookstore at **www.newharbinger.com** to order. Have your Visa or Mastercard number ready. Or send a check for the titles you want to New Harbinger Publications, Inc., 5674 Shattuck Ave., Oakland, CA 94609. Include $4.50 for the first book and 75¢ for each additional book, to cover shipping and handling. (California residents please include appropriate sales tax.) Allow two to five weeks for delivery.

Prices subject to change without notice.